React Native from Scratch

Build Cross-Platform Mobile Apps with JavaScript and Native Performance

Thompson Carter

Rafael Sanders

Miguel Farmer

[3]

Contents

Chapter 6: Navigating Between Screens in React Native 122

Chapter 7: Working with APIs in React Native 148

Chapter 9: State Management in React Native

Chapter 10: Debugging and Testing in React Native 228

Chapter 15: Next Steps and Advanced Topics 342

How to Scan a Barcode to Get a Repository

1. **Install a QR/Barcode Scanner** – Ensure you have a barcode or QR code scanner app installed on your smartphone or use a built-in scanner in **GitHub, GitLab, or Bitbucket.**

2. **Open the Scanner** – Launch the scanner app and grant necessary camera permissions.

3. **Scan the Barcode** – Align the barcode within the scanning frame. The scanner will automatically detect and process it.

4. **Follow the Link** – The scanned result will display a **URL to the repository.** Tap the link to open it in your web browser or Git client.

5. **Clone the Repository** – Use **Git clone** with the provided URL to download the repository to your local machine.

Chapter 1: Introduction to React Native

Overview of React Native and Its Benefits for Building Cross-Platform Mobile Apps

In today's fast-paced tech world, building mobile applications for multiple platforms (iOS and Android) used to mean writing separate codebases in different programming languages—Swift for iOS and Java for Android. This not only made development time-consuming but also increased the overall complexity of maintaining two different codebases.

Enter **React Native**, a groundbreaking framework that allows you to build mobile apps using **JavaScript** and **React**, enabling you to write a single codebase that works across both iOS and Android. This revolutionary framework was developed by **Facebook** in 2015 and has since become one of the most popular tools for mobile app development.

React Native provides the best of both worlds: You can build mobile apps that look and feel like native apps, while writing code once, saving time and resources. The key benefits of React Native include:

1. **Cross-Platform Development**: One of the most significant advantages is that React Native allows developers to write one codebase and deploy it to both iOS and Android. This reduces development time, costs, and complexity.

2. **Fast Development Cycle**: With **hot reloading**, developers can see changes instantly, making it easier to iterate and refine the app as development progresses.

3. **Native Performance**: Unlike other cross-platform frameworks, React Native provides near-native performance by using **native components** rather than web components, which results in smoother, faster apps.

4. **Large Community and Ecosystem**: Being an open-source project, React Native has a vibrant community of developers and

contributors. You can find a wealth of resources, plugins, and libraries to extend functionality without having to reinvent the wheel.

5. **Access to Native Modules**: React Native allows you to write platform-specific code when necessary, giving you the flexibility to integrate deeply with iOS and Android features, such as push notifications, camera access, and GPS.

6. **Cost-Effective**: Since you're building one codebase for multiple platforms, it's much cheaper and faster to maintain compared to having separate native codebases for iOS and Android.

Differences Between React Native and Traditional Native Development

Now that we've covered the basics of React Native, let's dive deeper into how it compares with traditional native development. If you've worked with **native mobile development** before, you may be accustomed to writing two separate codebases for iOS and Android using **Swift** (or Objective-C) for iOS and **Java/Kotlin** for Android.

Let's take a closer look at the key differences:

1. **Codebase:**

   o **Traditional Native Development:** You write two separate codebases— one in Swift/Objective-C for iOS, and the other in Java/Kotlin for Android.

- o **React Native:** One codebase written in JavaScript works for both iOS and Android. The framework uses **React** components that map to native views, so the app feels native on both platforms.

2. **Development Speed:**

- o **Traditional Native Development:** Since you are building two separate apps, the development process can take longer, especially when you need to make updates or fixes to both versions.

- o **React Native:** Faster development due to the shared codebase. You can use **hot reloading** to instantly see the changes made to the app without restarting it, which accelerates the development process.

3. **Performance:**

- o **Traditional Native Development:** Native apps are optimized for their respective platforms, giving them the best performance. The apps have direct access to device resources and hardware, which can result in better responsiveness, speed, and smoothness.

- o **React Native:** Although React Native provides native-like performance, it may not always match the performance of a truly native app, especially for complex animations and tasks that require intensive calculations. However, React Native has made significant improvements, and for most applications, performance is more than adequate.

4. **UI Components:**

   ○ **Traditional Native Development:** The UI is built using native components provided by the platform (e.g., **UIButton, UITextView** for iOS, or **Button, TextView** for Android).

   ○ **React Native:** React Native provides its own set of cross-platform components that map directly to native components under the hood. For example, you use <Text>, <View>, and <Button> elements, and React Native translates them to platform-specific components.

5. **Access to Native Modules:**

   ○ **Traditional Native Development:** Direct access to native APIs and device features is straightforward since you're working directly with the platform's native language.

o **React Native**: React Native allows you to integrate native code when needed via **native modules**. This allows you to access platform-specific APIs that are not available through React Native's built-in components. You can also integrate third-party libraries that wrap native code.

6. **Learning Curve**:

o **Traditional Native Development**: Learning Swift for iOS and Java for Android can be a steep learning curve, especially if you're new to programming.

o **React Native:** React Native allows developers with a background in **JavaScript** and **React** to easily transition into mobile development. React Native leverages JavaScript, one of the most widely used programming languages, making it accessible to a large pool of developers.

How to Set Up the Development Environment (Node.js, npm, React Native CLI, etc.)

Now that we have a better understanding of React Native and its advantages, let's set up the development environment to get started building our very first app.

Before diving into React Native development, you need to ensure that you have the required tools installed on your system. These include:

1. **Node.js**: React Native uses JavaScript, and Node.js allows you to run JavaScript outside the browser.

2. **npm (Node Package Manager)**: npm is the default package manager for Node.js, and it's used to install libraries and tools.

3. **React Native CLI**: This is a command-line tool that lets you create, build, and run React Native projects.

4. **Xcode (for iOS development)**: If you're building an iOS app, you'll need Xcode installed on a macOS machine.

5. **Android Studio (for Android development)**: If you're developing for

Android, you'll need Android Studio and its associated SDKs installed.

Step 1: Install Node.js and npm

1. Go to the Node.js website.

2. Download and install the **LTS version** of Node.js. This will include both **Node.js** and **npm**.

3. To verify the installation, open a terminal (or command prompt) and type:

```
nginx
```

```
node -v
npm -v
```

This will display the versions of Node.js and npm that are installed.

Step 2: Install React Native CLI

React Native can be installed via the command line interface (CLI). Here's how to set it up:

1. Open your terminal (or command prompt) and run the following command:

```
java
```

```
npm install -g react-native-cli
```

2. After installation, verify the CLI installation by typing:

```
css
```

```
react-native --version
```

Step 3: Set Up Xcode (for macOS users developing iOS apps)

If you're planning to develop for iOS, you'll need Xcode, which is available only for macOS.

1. Open the **Mac App Store** and search for **Xcode**.

2. Download and install Xcode.

3. After installation, open Xcode and agree to the terms and conditions.

Once you've set up Xcode, you should also install the **Xcode Command Line Tools**:

1. Open the terminal and type:

```
lua
```

```
xcode-select --install
```

Step 4: Set Up Android Studio

For Android development, you need to install Android Studio, which provides all the necessary tools for building Android apps.

1. Download Android Studio from the official website.

2. Follow the installation instructions to set up Android Studio.

3. Once installed, open Android Studio, and install the required SDKs and build tools.

Step 5: Create Your First React Native Project

Once you have your environment set up, you're ready to create your first React Native project. In your terminal, run:

```
csharp
```

```
react-native init MyFirstApp
```

This will create a new directory called MyFirstApp with all the necessary files for a React Native app.

To start the app on an Android or iOS emulator, navigate into the app's directory and run:

- For iOS (macOS only):

```
arduino
```

```
react-native run-ios
```

- For Android:

```
arduino
```

```
react-native run-android
```

Your first React Native app should now be up and running!

Conclusion

Congratulations! You've now learned the fundamentals of React Native, its advantages over traditional mobile development, and how to set up your development environment. You should now have a basic understanding of React Native's capabilities and be ready to dive deeper into building your first cross-platform app. React Native's ecosystem is vast, and by following along with this chapter, you've set the stage for creating apps that run seamlessly on both iOS and Android.

In the next chapter, we'll delve into the fundamentals of **JavaScript** and **React**, laying the groundwork for building more complex mobile apps with React Native. So roll up your sleeves, and get ready for an exciting journey into the world of mobile development with React Native!

Chapter 2: Understanding the Basics of JavaScript

Quick Refresher on JavaScript Fundamentals

Before we dive into React Native, it's important to have a solid understanding of **JavaScript**, the language that powers React Native. If you've already worked with JavaScript, this section will serve as a quick refresher. If you're new to the language, don't worry—by the end of this chapter, you'll feel comfortable with the basics and ready to move on to more advanced features.

JavaScript is a **scripting language** primarily used for creating dynamic content on the web, and it is one of the most widely used programming languages. It runs in the browser and on the server (using environments like **Node.js**), which makes it versatile for both client-side and server-side development. JavaScript is known for its ease of use, flexibility, and power.

Variables and Data Types

In JavaScript, we store values in **variables**. You can think of a variable as a box that holds a piece of data. JavaScript has three main ways to declare variables:

1. **var**: Older syntax used before ES6 (we'll get into this in a moment).

2. **let**: Introduced in ES6, this allows you to declare variables that can change later.

3. **const**: Also introduced in ES6, this is used for variables whose values can't be reassigned.

JavaScript also supports various **data types** including:

- **Primitive Types**:

  o **String**: 'Hello World'

  o **Number**: 42

  o **Boolean**: true or false

  o **Null**: A special value representing nothing (null)

- o **Undefined**: A variable that has been declared but not assigned a value (undefined)

- **Non-Primitive Types**:

  - o **Objects**: { key: 'value' }

  - o **Arrays**: ['apple', 'banana', 'cherry']

  - o **Functions**: Blocks of reusable code

Here's an example of declaring variables with different data types:

javascript

```
let name = "Alice";        // String
let age = 25;              // Number
let isStudent = true;      //
Boolean
let user = { name: 'Alice', age:
25 };  // Object
```

```javascript
let fruits = ['apple', 'banana',
'cherry'];  // Array
```

Control Flow: Conditionals and Loops

In JavaScript, control flow allows you to make decisions based on conditions and repeat actions multiple times using loops.

1. **Conditionals** (if-else statements): These are used to execute code only when certain conditions are true.

javascript

```javascript
let age = 20;
if (age >= 18) {
    console.log('You are an
adult.');
} else {
    console.log('You are a
minor.');
```

```
}
```

2. **Loops**: Loops allow you to run a block of code multiple times. The most common types of loops are **for loops** and **while loops.**

For Loop:

javascript

```javascript
for (let i = 0; i < 5; i++) {
    console.log(i);
}
```

While Loop:

javascript

```javascript
let i = 0;
while (i < 5) {
    console.log(i);
    i++;
}
```

Functions: Organizing Your Code

Functions are one of the core building blocks of JavaScript. A function allows you to encapsulate code into reusable blocks, making it easier to organize and maintain.

Here's a simple example of a function that adds two numbers:

```
javascript
```

```javascript
function add(a, b) {
    return a + b;
}


console.log(add(2, 3));   //
Output: 5
```

Functions can also be assigned to variables, which is particularly useful in React Native when working with events or callbacks.

```
javascript
```

```
let multiply = function(a, b) {
    return a * b;
};


console.log(multiply(2, 3));  //
Output: 6
```

ES6 Features That Are Essential for React Native Development

In recent years, JavaScript has evolved significantly with the introduction of **ES6** (ECMAScript 6), which brought many useful features that are essential for modern development. Here are some of the most important ES6 features that you'll use frequently in React Native.

1. Arrow Functions

One of the most popular features of ES6 is **arrow functions**. Arrow functions provide a shorter syntax for writing functions and automatically bind the this value (which can be tricky in JavaScript). They are especially useful when you are working with callbacks in React components.

Here's the traditional way of defining a function:

javascript

```javascript
function greet(name) {
    return 'Hello, ' + name + '!';
}
```

And here's how you can write it as an arrow function:

javascript

```javascript
const greet = (name) => 'Hello, '
+ name + '!';
```

Arrow functions make your code more concise and easier to read, and they're commonly used in React Native code.

2. Destructuring

Destructuring is a feature that allows you to unpack values from arrays or properties from objects into variables. This makes it much easier to work with complex data structures and improves code readability.

For example, instead of accessing object properties like this:

```javascript
let user = { name: 'Alice', age: 25 };
let name = user.name;
let age = user.age;
```

You can use **object destructuring** to unpack the values:

```
javascript
```

```
let { name, age } = user;
```

You can also destructure arrays:

```
javascript
```

```
let fruits = ['apple', 'banana',
'cherry'];
let [first, second] = fruits;
```

3. Promises

Promises are used to handle asynchronous operations in JavaScript. They represent an operation that will eventually complete (or fail) and provide a way to handle those results.

Here's an example of using a promise to fetch data from a server:

```
javascript
```

```
let fetchData = new
Promise((resolve, reject) => {
    let success = true;  //
Simulate whether the request is
successful

    if (success) {
        resolve('Data fetched
successfully!');
    } else {
        reject('Error fetching
data.');
    }
});

fetchData.then((result) => {
    console.log(result);  //
Output: Data fetched successfully!
}).catch((error) => {
    console.log(error);   //
Output: Error fetching data.
```

```
});
```

Promises are essential for handling asynchronous operations like **network requests** in React Native.

4. Async/Await

Async/await is a modern syntax for handling asynchronous code that makes working with promises even easier. With async/await, you can write asynchronous code that looks synchronous, which makes it much easier to read and understand.

Here's an example of how you can use **async/await** to handle a promise:

```javascript
async function fetchData() {
    let success = true;  //
Simulate whether the request is
successful
```

```
    if (success) {
        return 'Data fetched
successfully!';
    } else {
        throw new Error('Error
fetching data.');
    }
}


async function getData() {
    try {
        let result = await
fetchData();
        console.log(result);   //
Output: Data fetched successfully!
    } catch (error) {
        console.log(error);    //
Output: Error fetching data.
    }
}
```

```
getData();
```

Using async/await makes your asynchronous code easier to read and less prone to errors, which is crucial when working with React Native, where network requests and asynchronous code are common.

Setting Up Your First JavaScript Environment

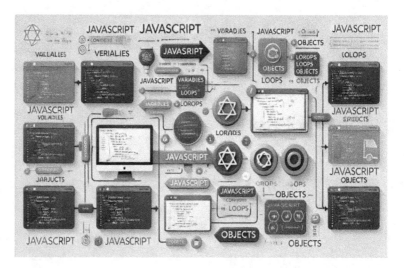

Now that you're familiar with the basic concepts of JavaScript, it's time to set up your first

JavaScript environment and start writing code. Don't worry—it's easier than you might think!

Step 1: Installing Node.js and npm

To get started with JavaScript development, you'll need to install **Node.js**, which comes with **npm** (Node Package Manager). npm is used to manage JavaScript libraries and tools.

1. Go to the Node.js website.

2. Download the **LTS version** (Long Term Support) and follow the installation instructions.

3. Once installed, open your terminal or command prompt and check the installation by running:

```bash
```

```
node -v
npm -v
```

This will print the version numbers of Node.js and npm.

Step 2: Setting Up a Simple Project

Now that you have Node.js and npm installed, let's set up a simple JavaScript project.

1. **Create a New Directory** for your project:

bash

```
mkdir my-first-project
cd my-first-project
```

2. **Initialize a New npm Project**: Run the following command to create a package.json file:

bash

```
npm init -y
```

3. **Create a JavaScript File**: Create a new file called index.js and open it in your code editor.

4. **Write Your First Code**: Open index.js and add the following code:

```javascript

console.log('Hello, JavaScript!');
```

5. **Run Your Code**: Go back to your terminal and run the code by typing:

```bash

node index.js
```

You should see the output: Hello, JavaScript!

Congratulations! You've just set up your first JavaScript environment and ran your first piece of code.

Conclusion

In this chapter, we covered the basics of **JavaScript**, including variables, control flow, functions, and some essential **ES6 features** like arrow functions, destructuring, promises, and async/await. These are fundamental concepts that will make your journey with React Native much smoother and more efficient.

We also set up your first JavaScript project, which is the first step toward building applications in React Native. With these foundations in place, you're now ready to dive deeper into more complex topics and begin building real-world apps.

In the next chapter, we'll explore **React**—how to work with components, props, and state—so you can start building interactive user interfaces with React Native. Keep practicing, and remember: JavaScript is your tool to create amazing things!

[55]

Chapter 3: Core Concepts of React

JSX Syntax: What It Is and How It Works

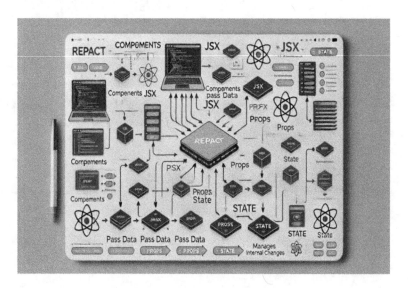

When you first look at React code, you'll notice something strange. Instead of traditional HTML or JavaScript, React uses something called **JSX** (JavaScript XML). If you're new to it, JSX might feel a little alien at first, but don't worry—it's easier to understand than it seems.

JSX is a syntax extension for JavaScript, allowing you to write HTML-like elements in your JavaScript code. JSX makes the process of creating user interfaces more intuitive and visually appealing by combining the power of JavaScript with the structure of HTML.

What Is JSX?

At its core, **JSX** is a way to write HTML-like code in JavaScript. React uses JSX to define the structure of a component. For example, here's what JSX looks like:

```jsx
const element = <h1>Hello,
world!</h1>;
```

This looks a lot like HTML, right? But it's not exactly HTML—it's actually JavaScript! In fact,

JSX gets transpiled (converted) into JavaScript that creates React elements. React components can be written in JSX, allowing you to declare the structure and behavior of your app in one place.

Why JSX?

JSX makes it easier to work with React because it provides a visual structure for your components. Imagine you're creating a to-do list app. With JSX, you can write the HTML structure of the app directly in JavaScript:

```jsx
function TodoApp() {
    return (
        <div>
            <h1>My Todo List</h1>
            <ul>
                <li>Learn
React</li>
```

```
            <li>Build a Todo
App</li>
            <li>Get a Job</li>
        </ul>
      </div>
    );
}
```

This component represents the UI of a to-do list app. The JSX syntax is easy to follow, and it clearly expresses the layout of the app. When React runs, it takes this JSX and turns it into a **React element,** which represents the DOM (Document Object Model) elements in the browser.

JSX Rules

While JSX might look like HTML, there are a few important rules to follow:

1. **JSX is an expression:** JSX is just a syntactic sugar for React.createElement(). It gets

transpiled into regular JavaScript code, so you can use it inside functions or expressions.

2. **HTML attributes**: In HTML, you write class, but in JSX, you use className because class is a reserved keyword in JavaScript.

3. **Self-closing tags**: In HTML, some tags can be self-closing (like <img />). In JSX, it's a requirement for these tags to be written as self-closing.

4. **Returning one element**: A React component must return a single root element. If you need multiple elements, wrap them in a parent element like <div> or use **Fragments**.

Here's an example of using **Fragments** to avoid unnecessary DOM elements:

[61]

```jsx
function TodoApp() {
    return (
        <>
            <h1>My Todo List</h1>
            <ul>
                <li>Learn React</li>
                <li>Build a Todo App</li>
                <li>Get a Job</li>
            </ul>
        </>
    );
}
```

Fragments allow you to return multiple elements without adding extra nodes to the DOM.

How JSX Gets Transformed

When you write JSX, it's not directly understood by browsers. React uses a tool called **Babel** to transform JSX into regular JavaScript. For example:

```jsx
const element = <h1>Hello, world!</h1>;
```

Babel transpiles it into the following JavaScript code:

```javascript
const element = React.createElement('h1', null, 'Hello, world!');
```

This process allows JSX to seamlessly integrate with JavaScript, enabling you to write code that's easier to understand while maintaining the power of JavaScript.

Components and Props

Now that we understand JSX, we can move on to one of the core concepts of React: **components.**

In React, **components** are reusable building blocks of your application. Components define how your app looks and behaves. There are two main types of components in React: **functional components** and **class components.**

Functional Components

Functional components are JavaScript functions that accept **props** (short for properties) as arguments and return JSX to render the UI. Here's an example of a simple functional component:

```jsx

function Welcome(props) {
    return <h1>Hello,
{props.name}</h1>;
}
```

In this example, the component **Welcome** accepts props as an argument, which contains data passed from a parent component. When you call this component and pass it a name prop, it will render the name dynamically:

```jsx

<Welcome name="Alice" />
```

This will render:

```html

<h1>Hello, Alice</h1>
```

Class Components

Class components are more traditional and use JavaScript classes. Here's the same **Welcome** component written as a class component:

jsx

```jsx
class Welcome extends
React.Component {
    render() {
        return <h1>Hello,
{this.props.name}</h1>;
    }
}
```

Class components can also have additional features like **state** (we'll get to that in the next section). While functional components are now favored due to their simplicity, class components are still commonly used and understood.

Props: Passing Data to Components

In React, **props** allow you to pass data from a parent component to a child component. Props are **immutable**, meaning they cannot be modified by the child component. They're simply passed down as data for rendering.

Let's say we want to pass a list of items to a TodoList component:

jsx

```
function TodoList(props) {
    return (
        <ul>
            {props.todos.map(todo
=> <li key={todo}>{todo}</li>)}
        </ul>
    );
}
```

Now, we can pass an array of todos
from the parent component:
jsx

```
function App() {
    const todos = ['Learn React',
'Build a Todo App', 'Get a Job'];
    return <TodoList todos={todos}
/>;
}
```

This allows the parent to control the data and pass it down to the child for rendering. The TodoList component renders the list of todos dynamically, showing the power and flexibility of props.

Best Practices for Props

- **Destructure props**: Instead of accessing props as props.name, you can destructure them for cleaner code:

```jsx
function Welcome({ name }) {
    return <h1>Hello, {name}</h1>;
}
```

- **Default props:** If a prop is not passed, you can define a default value:

```jsx
Welcome.defaultProps = {
    name: 'Guest',
};
```

State and Lifecycle Methods

Now that you understand **JSX** and props, the next key concept is **state**. In React, **state** is used to track data that can change over time, like user input, **API** responses, or animations.

What Is State?

State represents data that can change within a component. Unlike props, which are passed down from a parent, **state** is managed within the component itself.

Here's an example of a component with state:

jsx

```jsx
class Counter extends
React.Component {
    constructor(props) {
        super(props);
        this.state = {
            count: 0,
        };
    }


    increment = () => {
        this.setState({ count:
this.state.count + 1 });
```

```
    };


    render() {
        return (
            <div>

<h1>{this.state.count}</h1>
                <button
onClick={this.increment}>Increment
</button>
            </div>
        );
    }
}
```

In this example, the Counter component has a state variable count, which is initialized to 0. When the user clicks the **Increment** button, the state is updated, and React re-renders the component with the new value.

Managing State in Functional Components with Hooks

With the introduction of **React Hooks** in React 16.8, managing state in functional components became possible. Here's how you can use the useState hook:

```jsx

import React, { useState } from
'react';
```

```
function Counter() {
    const [count, setCount] =
useState(0);

    const increment = () => {
        setCount(count + 1);
    };

    return (
        <div>
            <h1>{count}</h1>
            <button
onClick={increment}>Increment</but
ton>
        </div>
    );
}
```

This version of the Counter component uses the useState hook to handle the state. You get two things back from useState: the current state value (count) and a function (setCount) to update it.

Lifecycle Methods

React components go through several stages, and during these stages, you may want to perform specific actions. These stages are known as the **component lifecycle**. In class components, you have access to various **lifecycle methods** to manage these stages.

For example, the componentDidMount method is called after a component is rendered for the first time:

```jsx
class App extends React.Component
{
    componentDidMount() {
        console.log('App has
mounted!');
    }
}
```

```
render() {
    return <h1>Hello,
World!</h1>;
    }
}
```

In functional components, lifecycle methods are replaced by **Hooks** like useEffect, which runs after the component renders. Here's how you can use the useEffect hook:

jsx

```
import React, { useEffect } from 'react';

function App() {
    useEffect(() => {
        console.log('App has mounted!');
```

```
}, []); // Empty array means
it runs only once, after the first
render


    return <h1>Hello, World!</h1>;
}
```

Best Practices for State and Lifecycle Methods

- **Avoid direct state mutation**: Always use this.setState() (class components) or the state setter function (functional components) to update state. Directly modifying the state will not trigger a re-render.

- **Use lifecycle methods and hooks wisely**: Lifecycle methods and hooks are powerful, but they can lead to bugs if used improperly. Always consider whether your component should manage state or rely on props, and try to keep side effects like data fetching inside useEffect or componentDidMount.

Conclusion

In this chapter, we've explored the core concepts of React, including **JSX**, **components and props**, and **state and lifecycle methods**. These concepts form the foundation of React development, and understanding them will enable you to create dynamic, interactive user interfaces with React.

By now, you should feel comfortable with JSX syntax, how to pass data with props, how to manage state within components, and how to work with lifecycle methods. With these tools at your disposal, you're well on your way to building powerful React applications!

In the next chapter, we'll dive into **Event Handling** and **Forms**, two essential aspects of building interactive applications with React. Keep experimenting and building, and remember: React is all about breaking down your app into small, manageable components—one step at a time!

Chapter 4: Getting Started with React Native

Introduction to React Native Components

When you're building apps with React Native, you'll be working with a set of **core components** that are essential for constructing the user interface (UI). React Native provides several built-in components that represent common UI elements, such as **Text, View, Image**, and **ScrollView**, among others. These components allow you to define the structure of your app's interface.

Let's break down these essential components:

1. Text

The <Text> component is one of the most fundamental components in React Native. It's used for displaying text in your app.

Here's how you use the <Text> component:

```jsx
import React from 'react';
import { Text } from 'react-native';

export default function App() {
    return (
```

```
    <Text>Hello, welcome to
React Native!</Text>
    );
}
```

This simple example will display the text "Hello, welcome to React Native!" on the screen. The <Text> component allows you to style text, handle different font sizes, and even link text in a clickable manner.

2. View

The <View> component serves as a container for other components. It is analogous to a <div> in traditional web development. You can use the <View> component to structure the layout of your app by grouping related elements together.

Example:

```
jsx
```

```
import React from 'react';
```

```
import { View, Text } from 'react-
native';

export default function App() {
    return (
        <View style={{ padding: 20
}}>
            <Text>Hello, this is
inside a View!</Text>
        </View>
    );
}
```

Here, the <View> component acts as a wrapper for the <Text> component, and we've added some padding to create space inside the container.

3. Image

The <Image> component is used for displaying images in your app. React Native supports both local and remote images. To use the <Image>

component, you'll provide it with a source, which could be a file path (for local images) or a URL (for remote images).

Example for a local image:

jsx

```
import React from 'react';
import { View, Image } from
'react-native';

export default function App() {
    return (
        <View>
            <Image
source={require('./assets/logo.png
')} style={{ width: 200, height:
200 }} />
        </View>
    );
}
```

For remote images, use a URL as the source:

jsx

```
import React from 'react';
import { View, Image } from
'react-native';

export default function App() {
    return (
        <View>
            <Image source={{ uri:
'https://example.com/logo.png' }}
style={{ width: 200, height: 200
}} />
        </View>
    );
}
```

4. ScrollView

The <ScrollView> component is used when the content inside your app may be longer than the screen, so you need to make it scrollable. This component allows you to wrap content that exceeds the screen's height and make it scrollable vertically or horizontally.

Example:

```jsx
import React from 'react';
import { ScrollView, Text } from
'react-native';

export default function App() {
    return (
        <ScrollView style={{
padding: 20 }}>
            <Text>Scroll
me!</Text>
            <Text>Keep
scrolling...</Text>
```

```
        <Text>There's a lot of
content here.</Text>
        <Text>And more
content...</Text>
        </ScrollView>
    );
}
```

By wrapping the content in a <ScrollView>, you allow users to scroll through the content, ensuring that it's accessible on smaller screens.

Layout Basics: Flexbox, Padding, Margin

Layout in React Native is built on the **Flexbox** layout model. This makes it easier to build responsive layouts that adjust dynamically to different screen sizes. Understanding how to use Flexbox, along with padding and margin, is crucial to building flexible and well-structured apps.

1. Flexbox

Flexbox is a powerful layout system that allows you to create flexible and responsive layouts. The core concept of Flexbox is that elements inside a container can **flex** (resize) to fit the available space. React Native uses Flexbox by default for all components.

Here are the key properties used in Flexbox:

- **flexDirection**: Determines the main axis direction (horizontal or vertical).

  - row: Elements are arranged horizontally.

  - column: Elements are arranged vertically.

- **justifyContent**: Aligns children along the main axis (horizontal or vertical).

  - ○ flex-start: Aligns items to the start.

  - ○ center: Centers items.

  - ○ space-between: Distributes items evenly with space between them.

- **alignItems**: Aligns children along the cross axis (perpendicular to the main axis).

  - ○ flex-start: Aligns to the start.

  - ○ center: Aligns in the center.

  - ○ stretch: Stretches items to fill the container.

- **flex**: Defines how a component will grow relative to other components inside the container.

Example of Flexbox layout:

```jsx

import React from 'react';
import { View, Text } from 'react-native';

export default function App() {
    return (
        <View style={{ flex: 1, flexDirection: 'row', justifyContent: 'center', alignItems: 'center' }}>
            <Text style={{ flex: 1 }}>Item 1</Text>
            <Text style={{ flex: 1 }}>Item 2</Text>
            <Text style={{ flex: 1 }}>Item 3</Text>
        </View>
    );
}
```

In this example, the <View> container has a flexDirection: 'row', so the items are arranged horizontally. The justifyContent: 'center' property centers the items along the horizontal axis, and alignItems: 'center' centers them vertically within the container.

2. Padding and Margin

Padding and margin are used to control the spacing inside and outside of elements, respectively.

- **Padding**: Adds space inside the element, between the content and the border.

- **Margin**: Adds space outside the element, between it and other elements.

Example of using padding and margin:

jsx

```
import React from 'react';
```

```
import { View, Text } from 'react-
native';


export default function App() {
    return (
        <View style={{ flex: 1,
padding: 20 }}>
            <Text style={{
marginBottom: 10 }}>First item
with margin</Text>
            <Text>Second item with
padding</Text>
        </View>
    );
}
```

In this example:

- The <View> container has padding: 20, so all its child components will have a 20px space inside the container.

- The first <Text> component has marginBottom: 10, which gives a 10px space below it.

3. Responsive Layout with Flexbox

Flexbox helps in creating responsive layouts, where items adapt to different screen sizes. This is particularly useful for building mobile apps, where screen sizes vary across devices.

Example of a responsive layout:

```jsx
import React from 'react';
import { View, Text } from 'react-native';

export default function App() {
    return (
        <View style={{ flex: 1,
flexDirection: 'row',
```

```
justifyContent: 'space-around',
alignItems: 'center' }}>
        <Text style={{ flex: 1
}}>First item</Text>
        <Text style={{ flex: 1
}}>Second item</Text>
        <Text style={{ flex: 1
}}>Third item</Text>
    </View>
  );
}
```

Here, the three items inside the <View> will automatically resize and adjust depending on the screen size, thanks to the use of flex: 1 and justifyContent: 'space-around'.

Writing and Running Your First React Native App

Now that you have a good understanding of the core components and layout techniques, it's time to write and run your first React Native app! Don't worry; we'll take it step by step.

Step 1: Install React Native CLI

To start building React Native apps, you'll need to install the **React Native CLI**. This tool allows you to create and manage React Native projects from the command line.

1. **Install Node.js and npm**: First, you need Node.js and npm installed on your system (refer to Chapter 2 for setup details).

2. **Install React Native CLI**:

Open your terminal and run:

bash

```
npm install -g react-native-cli
```

Step 2: Initialize Your Project

Once the React Native CLI is installed, you can create your first project.

1. Open your terminal and run the following command:

bash

```
react-native init MyFirstApp
```

This will create a new React Native project called MyFirstApp.

2. Navigate into the newly created project folder:

```
bash
```

```
cd MyFirstApp
```

Step 3: Run Your App on an Emulator

Now that your project is created, you can run it on an Android or iOS emulator.

- **For iOS (macOS only):**

```
bash
```

```
react-native run-ios
```

- **For Android:**

Make sure you have an Android emulator running and use the following command:

```bash

```

```
react-native run-android
```

If everything is set up correctly, your app will launch in the emulator, and you'll see the default "Welcome to React Native" screen!

Conclusion

In this chapter, we covered the core components in React Native, including **Text**, **View**, **Image**, and **ScrollView**. We also discussed the basics of **layout** with Flexbox, padding, and margin, and we showed you how to structure a responsive layout that adjusts to different screen sizes.

Finally, we walked through the process of setting up your first React Native project and running it on an emulator. Now that you've built your first app, you're well on your way to becoming proficient in React Native development!

In the next chapter, we'll dive into **Event Handling** and **Forms** in React Native, where you'll learn how to capture user input and handle interactions in your app. Keep experimenting and building, and remember: React Native is all about creating flexible, powerful apps with minimal code!

Chapter 5: Styling in React Native

StyleSheet API and How It Works

Styling in React Native is an essential part of creating user interfaces that are both functional and visually appealing. Unlike web development, where styles are applied using **CSS**, React Native uses the **StyleSheet API** to handle styles. The

StyleSheet API is a built-in tool that allows you to define and manage styles for your components.

React Native styles are written in JavaScript and are essentially **objects** that represent the design of your UI elements. This is different from CSS, where styles are defined using a syntax that is specific to HTML. React Native's approach, using JavaScript objects for styles, makes it easier to manage styles programmatically.

1. What is the StyleSheet API?

The **StyleSheet API** is a core component in React Native that helps to define and apply styles to components. The API is used to create a **StyleSheet** object, which contains a set of styles that can be applied to various components. Once you define your styles in a StyleSheet, you can reference these styles in the component's JSX.

Here's an example of how to use the **StyleSheet** API:

```jsx
import React from 'react';
import { View, Text, StyleSheet }
from 'react-native';

export default function App() {
    return (
        <View
style={styles.container}>
            <Text
style={styles.text}>Welcome to
React Native Styling!</Text>
        </View>
    );
}

const styles = StyleSheet.create({
    container: {
```

```
    flex: 1,
    justifyContent: 'center',
    alignItems: 'center',
    backgroundColor:
'#f0f0f0',
  },
  text: {
    fontSize: 20,
    color: '#333',
  },
});
```

In this example:

- We create a styles object using StyleSheet.create().

- The container style sets up the layout, positioning, and background color for the container View.

- The text style controls the font size and color for the Text component.

The **StyleSheet.create()** method optimizes the styles and ensures they are rendered more efficiently by React Native.

2. Benefits of Using StyleSheet API

- **Performance**: The StyleSheet API is more efficient than using inline styles in React Native. It optimizes the styles to make them faster and more performant, especially in large applications.

- **Consistency**: Using the StyleSheet API ensures that styles are centralized, making it easier to maintain consistency across the app.

- **Readability**: The StyleSheet object allows you to group styles logically and makes it easier to read and manage styles in your app.

Styling Techniques and Best Practices

In React Native, styling is much like web development, but with a few key differences due to the mobile platform constraints. Let's explore some techniques and best practices to ensure that your styling is effective, responsive, and maintainable.

1. Using Flexbox for Layouts

As we covered earlier, **Flexbox** is the default layout system in React Native, making it easy to create flexible and responsive layouts. Flexbox works by distributing space inside a container, allowing child components to grow, shrink, or wrap based on the available space.

Here's how you can use Flexbox for a layout:

```
jsx
```

```
import React from 'react';
import { View, Text, StyleSheet }
from 'react-native';


export default function App() {
    return (
        <View
style={styles.container}>
            <Text
style={styles.item}>Item 1</Text>
            <Text
style={styles.item}>Item 2</Text>
            <Text
style={styles.item}>Item 3</Text>
        </View>
    );
}


const styles = StyleSheet.create({
    container: {
        flex: 1,
```

```
    flexDirection: 'row', //
Arrange items horizontally
    justifyContent: 'space-
between', // Distribute items
evenly
    padding: 10,
  },
  item: {
    backgroundColor:
'#4CAF50',
    padding: 10,
    color: 'white',
    flex: 1, // Each item will
take up equal space
  },
});
```

2. Managing Padding and Margin

- **Padding**: Adds space inside a component (between the component's content and its border).

- **Margin**: Adds space outside a component (between the component and other elements).

When you style components, it's crucial to balance padding and margin to avoid overcrowding or unnecessary whitespace.

Example:

```jsx
import React from 'react';
import { View, Text, StyleSheet }
from 'react-native';

export default function App() {
    return (
        <View
style={styles.container}>
```

```
        <Text
style={styles.text}>Hello,
world!</Text>
        </View>
    );
}


const styles = StyleSheet.create({
    container: {
        flex: 1,
        justifyContent: 'center',
        alignItems: 'center',
    },
    text: {
        padding: 20,
        margin: 10,
        backgroundColor:
'#8e44ad',
        color: 'white',
    },
});
```

In this example:

- The Text component has both padding and margin to control the inner and outer spacing respectively.

- Padding inside the Text ensures the text isn't too close to the edges of the component, and margin creates space between the Text and the View container.

3. Avoid Inline Styles

Using inline styles directly in JSX can quickly make your code messy and harder to maintain. Instead, define styles in a separate **StyleSheet** object. This is especially important in larger projects, where multiple components share similar styles.

Example of bad practice:

```
jsx
```

```jsx
<View style={{ flex: 1,
justifyContent: 'center',
alignItems: 'center' }}>
    <Text>Welcome to React
Native!</Text>
</View>
```

Example of good practice:
jsx

```jsx
const styles = StyleSheet.create({
    container: {
        flex: 1,
        justifyContent: 'center',
        alignItems: 'center',
    },
});
```

```jsx
<View style={styles.container}>
    <Text>Welcome to React
Native!</Text>
</View>
```

By using the StyleSheet API, we improve performance and maintainability.

4. Using Colors and Themes

It's a good practice to define colors as constants or in a separate theme file, especially if your app has a consistent color palette. This approach improves readability and consistency across your app.

Example:

jsx

```
const colors = {
    primary: '#4CAF50',
    secondary: '#FFC107',
    background: '#f0f0f0',
};

const styles = StyleSheet.create({
    container: {
```

```
    flex: 1,
    backgroundColor:
colors.background,
  },
  button: {
    backgroundColor:
colors.primary,
    padding: 15,
    borderRadius: 5,
  },
});
```

By centralizing your color scheme, you can easily update colors in the future without searching through every style in your app.

5. Using Percentage-Based Width and Height

Sometimes, it's beneficial to use percentage-based values for width and height to create responsive layouts. This allows components to resize dynamically based on the screen size.

Example:

```jsx
const styles = StyleSheet.create({
    container: {
        flex: 1,
        justifyContent: 'center',
        alignItems: 'center',
    },
    box: {
        width: '80%', // 80% of the screen width
        height: 200,
        backgroundColor: '#f39c12',
    },
});
```

This ensures the box always takes up 80% of the screen width, making your app more responsive across devices.

Handling Responsive Design with Flexbox

Building a responsive app is crucial for React Native development. Mobile screens come in different sizes and resolutions, so it's important to design flexible layouts that adapt to various devices. Thankfully, **Flexbox** makes it easier to build these responsive layouts.

1. Using Flexbox for Different Screen Sizes

Flexbox works well for creating layouts that adjust dynamically based on the screen size. By combining **flexDirection**, **justifyContent**, and **alignItems**, you can create flexible and responsive UI components.

Example of a responsive layout:

```jsx
import React from 'react';
import { View, Text, StyleSheet }
from 'react-native';

export default function App() {
    return (
        <View
style={styles.container}>
```

```
        <Text
style={styles.item}>First
item</Text>
        <Text
style={styles.item}>Second
item</Text>
        <Text
style={styles.item}>Third
item</Text>
    </View>
  );
}

const styles = StyleSheet.create({
    container: {
        flex: 1,
        flexDirection: 'row',
        justifyContent: 'space-
between',
        alignItems: 'center',
        padding: 10,
```

```
    },
    item: {
        flex: 1,
        backgroundColor:
'#8e44ad',
        padding: 20,
        color: 'white',
        margin: 5,
    },
});
```

In this example, the layout adjusts based on the screen size, with the flexDirection: 'row' arranging items horizontally and justifyContent: 'space-between' distributing space evenly.

2. Using Media Queries for Responsiveness

React Native doesn't support CSS media queries, but you can achieve similar results by using **Dimensions** and **useWindowDimensions**. These

APIs allow you to check the screen size and adjust the layout accordingly.

Example of using **Dimensions**:

```jsx
import React from 'react';
import { View, Text, StyleSheet,
Dimensions } from 'react-native';

const { width, height } =
Dimensions.get('window');

export default function App() {
    return (
        <View
style={styles.container}>
            <Text
style={styles.text}>Screen width:
{width}</Text>
```

```
        <Text
style={styles.text}>Screen height:
{height}</Text>
        </View>
    );
}


const styles = StyleSheet.create({
    container: {
        flex: 1,
        justifyContent: 'center',
        alignItems: 'center',
        backgroundColor:
'#f0f0f0',
    },
    text: {
        fontSize: 18,
        color: '#333',
    },
});
```

In this example, you can use the screen width and height to adjust the layout or apply conditional styling based on the device dimensions.

3. Scaling Units for Different Screen Densities

To make sure your app looks good on all devices, React Native provides an API called **PixelRatio**. This API allows you to scale units to match different screen densities.

Example:

```jsx
import { PixelRatio, Text } from
'react-native';

const scale = PixelRatio.get();

const styles = {
    text: {
```

```
    fontSize: 14 * scale, //
Scale font size based on the
screen density
    },
};
```

This ensures that your text and other elements scale appropriately on different devices, improving the user experience.

Conclusion

In this chapter, we've explored styling in React Native, focusing on the **StyleSheet API**, best practices for styling components, and how to handle responsive design using **Flexbox** and device dimensions.

By understanding how to use the **StyleSheet API** and implementing best practices like managing spacing, using Flexbox for layout, and incorporating responsive techniques, you're equipped to create visually appealing and adaptable mobile apps.

As you continue building your React Native apps, keep experimenting with different styles, layouts, and responsiveness techniques to refine your skills and make your apps shine on every device!

In the next chapter, we'll dive into **Event Handling and Forms**, where you'll learn how to manage user input and interactions in your React Native apps. Keep building, and remember: styling is an art, so take your time to perfect it!

Chapter 6: Navigating Between Screens in React Native

React Navigation Basics: Stack, Tab, and Drawer Navigators

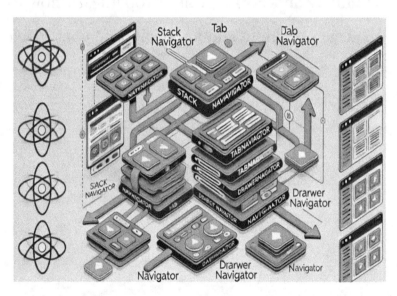

In most mobile applications, you'll need to move between different screens or views. React Native offers **React Navigation**, a powerful library that allows you to manage navigation between screens in your application. Understanding how to use different types of navigators is key to building fluid and intuitive mobile apps.

There are several navigators in React Navigation, but for this chapter, we will focus on three main types:

1. **Stack Navigator**

2. **Tab Navigator**

3. **Drawer Navigator**

Let's dive into each one and understand how to use them effectively.

1. Stack Navigator

The **Stack Navigator** is one of the most common types of navigators in React Native. It is based on a **stack** data structure, where each screen is pushed onto the stack, and when the user presses the back button, the top screen is popped off. This behavior mimics the way navigation works in native mobile apps.

How Stack Navigator Works

In a **Stack Navigator**, each screen is pushed onto the navigation stack, and the user can navigate forward and backward between screens. The Stack Navigator is ideal for simple navigation flows like login/signup screens, detail pages, and so on.

To get started, install the necessary dependencies:

bash

```
npm install @react-
navigation/native @react-
navigation/stack react-native-
screens react-native-safe-area-
context
```

Example of Stack Navigator

Let's set up a simple stack navigator with two screens: HomeScreen and DetailsScreen.

```jsx
import React from 'react';
import { Button, View, Text } from
'react-native';
import { NavigationContainer }
from '@react-navigation/native';
import { createStackNavigator }
from '@react-navigation/stack';

// HomeScreen component
function HomeScreen({ navigation
}) {
    return (
        <View>
            <Text>Welcome to the
Home Screen!</Text>
```

```
          <Button
            title="Go to
Details"
            onPress={() =>
navigation.navigate('Details')}
          />
        </View>
    );
}


// DetailsScreen component
function DetailsScreen() {
    return (
        <View>
            <Text>Welcome to the
Details Screen!</Text>
        </View>
    );
}


// Create the Stack Navigator
```

```
const Stack =
createStackNavigator();


// App component
export default function App() {
    return (
        <NavigationContainer>
            <Stack.Navigator
initialRouteName="Home">
                <Stack.Screen
name="Home" component={HomeScreen}
/>
                <Stack.Screen
name="Details"
component={DetailsScreen} />
            </Stack.Navigator>
        </NavigationContainer>
    );
}
```

Explanation

1. We create two simple screens: HomeScreen and DetailsScreen.

2. The HomeScreen has a button that uses navigation.navigate('Details') to navigate to the DetailsScreen.

3. We wrap the Stack.Navigator inside the NavigationContainer, which is essential for navigation in React Native apps.

In this example, when the user clicks on the "Go to Details" button, the app navigates to the DetailsScreen. The stack navigator allows users to go back to the HomeScreen by using the back gesture or the back button.

2. Tab Navigator

The **Tab Navigator** is another useful type of navigator, especially for apps with multiple top-level screens. It allows users to switch between different sections of your app using tabs (similar to the tabs found in many apps like Instagram or Twitter).

How Tab Navigator Works

A **Tab Navigator** allows you to create a tab-based navigation experience. It's ideal for apps that need to switch between different categories or sections, like Home, Profile, and Settings.

To get started with the Tab Navigator, you'll need to install:

bash

npm install @react-navigation/bottom-tabs

Example of Tab Navigator

Let's set up a simple app with three tabs: Home, Search, and Profile.

jsx

```
import React from 'react';
import { Text, View } from 'react-
native';
import { NavigationContainer }
from '@react-navigation/native';
import { createBottomTabNavigator
} from '@react-navigation/bottom-
tabs';

// HomeScreen component
function HomeScreen() {
    return (
        <View>
            <Text>Home
Screen</Text>
        </View>
    );
}

// SearchScreen component
function SearchScreen() {
```

```
    return (
        <View>
            <Text>Search
Screen</Text>
        </View>
    );
}


// ProfileScreen component
function ProfileScreen() {
    return (
        <View>
            <Text>Profile
Screen</Text>
        </View>
    );
}


// Create the Tab Navigator
const Tab =
createBottomTabNavigator();
```

```
// App component
export default function App() {
    return (
        <NavigationContainer>
            <Tab.Navigator
initialRouteName="Home">
                <Tab.Screen
name="Home" component={HomeScreen}
/>
                <Tab.Screen
name="Search"
component={SearchScreen} />
                <Tab.Screen
name="Profile"
component={ProfileScreen} />
            </Tab.Navigator>
        </NavigationContainer>
    );
}
```

Explanation

1. We define three simple screens: HomeScreen, SearchScreen, and ProfileScreen.

2. The Tab.Navigator component is used to create a bottom tab bar that allows users to switch between the three screens.

3. The initialRouteName="Home" prop ensures that the Home tab is selected first when the app is loaded.

3. Drawer Navigator

The **Drawer Navigator** is another type of navigation that provides a sliding menu (drawer) that can be accessed from the side of the screen. This is useful for apps that require access to many different sections or features in a compact space.

How Drawer Navigator Works

The **Drawer Navigator** allows users to swipe from the left (or right) to open a side menu with a list of options. This is often used for app menus, like navigation drawers in Gmail or Facebook apps.

To use the Drawer Navigator, install:

bash

```
npm install @react-
navigation/drawer
```

Example of Drawer Navigator

Let's create a basic drawer navigator with three sections: Home, Settings, and Profile.

jsx

```
import React from 'react';
import { Text, View } from 'react-
native';
import { NavigationContainer }
from '@react-navigation/native';
import { createDrawerNavigator }
from '@react-navigation/drawer';
```

```
// HomeScreen component
function HomeScreen() {
    return (
        <View>
            <Text>Home
Screen</Text>
        </View>
    );
}


// SettingsScreen component
function SettingsScreen() {
    return (
        <View>
            <Text>Settings
Screen</Text>
        </View>
    );
}
```

```
// ProfileScreen component
function ProfileScreen() {
    return (
        <View>
            <Text>Profile
Screen</Text>
        </View>
    );
}


// Create the Drawer Navigator
const Drawer =
createDrawerNavigator();


// App component
export default function App() {
    return (
        <NavigationContainer>
            <Drawer.Navigator
initialRouteName="Home">
```

```
                <Drawer.Screen
name="Home" component={HomeScreen}
/>
                  <Drawer.Screen
name="Settings"
component={SettingsScreen} />
                  <Drawer.Screen
name="Profile"
component={ProfileScreen} />
          </Drawer.Navigator>
        </NavigationContainer>
      );
}
```

Explanation

1. We define three screens: HomeScreen, SettingsScreen, and ProfileScreen.

2. The Drawer.Navigator creates a sliding drawer navigation with a menu for each screen.

3. The user can open the drawer by swiping from the left edge of the screen or by clicking the hamburger menu (three lines icon) in the top left corner.

Passing Data Between Screens and Managing Navigation State

In most mobile apps, you'll need to pass data between screens, whether it's user preferences, results from an API call, or any other state that needs to be shared. React Navigation allows you to pass data easily between screens and manage navigation state.

1. Passing Parameters to Screens

You can pass parameters from one screen to another using the navigate method. These parameters can be accessed in the destination screen's props.

Example of passing parameters:

```jsx
function HomeScreen({ navigation }) {
    return (
        <View>
            <Button
                title="Go to Details"
```

```
                onPress={() =>
navigation.navigate('Details', {
itemId: 42 })}
        />
    </View>
    );
}


function DetailsScreen({ route })
{
    const { itemId } =
route.params;
    return (
        <View>
            <Text>Details for item
{itemId}</Text>
        </View>
    );
}
```

Explanation

- In the HomeScreen, we pass an itemId parameter to the DetailsScreen when navigating using navigation.navigate('Details', { itemId: 42 }).

- In the DetailsScreen, we access the itemId parameter using route.params.

2. Managing Navigation State

React Navigation allows you to manage the navigation state by using **navigation listeners** and **state**.

For example, you can track whether a screen is focused or not:

```jsx
import { useFocusEffect } from
'@react-navigation/native';

function MyComponent() {
```

```
useFocusEffect(
    React.useCallback(() => {
        console.log('Screen is
focused!');
        return () => {

console.log('Screen is
unfocused!');
        };
    }, [])
  );
    return <View><Text>Check the
console!</Text></View>;
}
```

This allows you to execute specific actions when a screen comes into focus or loses focus.

Deep Linking and Handling the Back Button on Android

Deep linking allows users to open specific pages within your app from outside the app, such as from a URL in a browser or an email link. React Navigation supports deep linking to handle these types of links.

1. Deep Linking

To enable deep linking in React Native, you need to configure the app to handle external links and map those links to specific screens in your app.

Example of deep linking setup:

```jsx
import { Linking } from 'react-native';
import { NavigationContainer }
from '@react-navigation/native';
```

```
const linking = {
    prefixes: ['myapp://'],
    config: {
        screens: {
            Home: '',
            Details:
'details/:id',
        },
    },
};

export default function App() {
    return (
        <NavigationContainer
linking={linking}>
            {/* Your navigator
here */}
        </NavigationContainer>
    );
}
```

In this example:

- We define a deep link prefix (myapp://).

- The Details screen can be accessed via a URL like myapp://details/42, where 42 is a dynamic parameter.

2. Handling the Back Button on Android

Handling the back button on Android devices is a crucial part of building mobile apps. React Navigation provides a way to intercept and manage the back button behavior.

Example:

jsx

```
import { BackHandler } from
'react-native';
```

```
function
useCustomBackHandler(navigation) {
    React.useEffect(() => {
        const backAction = () => {
            navigation.goBack();
            return true;
        };

        const backHandler =
BackHandler.addEventListener('hard
wareBackPress', backAction);

        return () => {
            backHandler.remove();
        };
    }, [navigation]);
}
```

This custom hook allows you to intercept the back button press and navigate to the previous screen, or perform any other custom behavior.

Conclusion

In this chapter, we explored the basics of **React Navigation**, covering key navigators such as **Stack**, **Tab**, and **Drawer**. We also discussed how to pass data between screens, manage navigation state, and handle deep linking and back button events.

By understanding how to use these navigation tools effectively, you can create fluid, interactive, and user-friendly navigation flows in your React Native apps. In the next chapter, we'll dive deeper into **Event Handling** and **Forms** to enhance user interactivity and data handling in your app. Keep exploring and remember, navigation is the backbone of any app's usability!

Chapter 7: Working with APIs in React Native

Introduction

In modern mobile app development, fetching data from external sources is a common task. Whether it's retrieving user data, fetching news articles, or pulling information from an external service, APIs (Application Programming Interfaces) are a crucial part of mobile applications. React Native makes it easy to work with APIs by offering built-in tools like fetch and popular third-party libraries like **Axios**.

In this chapter, we will dive deep into the process of working with APIs in React Native. You will learn:

1. How to fetch data from APIs using both fetch and Axios.

2. How to display dynamic data in components.

3. How to handle errors and manage loading states during data fetching.

Whether you're a beginner, hobbyist, or professional, this chapter will guide you through the concepts and provide actionable insights that you can apply to your projects.

1. Fetching Data Using Fetch and Axios

Fetching data from an API is one of the most common tasks in mobile app development. In React Native, there are two primary ways to make HTTP requests: using the native fetch function or using the popular Axios library.

Using fetch

The fetch function is a built-in JavaScript function that allows you to make network requests to retrieve data from an API. It is a Promise-based API, meaning you can use .then() and .catch() to handle responses and errors.

Here's an example of how to use fetch to get data from a public API:

```javascript
```

```
import React, { useState,
useEffect } from 'react';
import { View, Text,
ActivityIndicator } from 'react-
native';

const API_URL =
'https://jsonplaceholder.typicode.
com/posts';

export default function App() {
    const [data, setData] =
useState([]);
    const [loading, setLoading] =
useState(true);
    const [error, setError] =
useState(null);

    useEffect(() => {
        // Fetch data from the API
        fetch(API_URL)
```

```
        .then(response =>
response.json()) // Parse the JSON
from the response
            .then(jsonData => {
            setData(jsonData);
// Store data in state
                setLoading(false);
// Set loading state to false once
data is fetched
            })
            .catch(err => {
                setError(err); //
Set error state if there's an
issue with the fetch request
                setLoading(false);
// Set loading state to false in
case of an error
            });
    }, []); // Empty array ensures
this effect runs once on component
mount
```

```
if (loading) {
    return <ActivityIndicator
size="large" color="#0000ff" />;
}

if (error) {
    return <Text>Error:
{error.message}</Text>;
}

return (
    <View style={{ padding: 20
}}>
        <Text style={{
fontSize: 20, marginBottom: 10
}}>Fetched Posts:</Text>
        {data.map(item => (
            <View
key={item.id} style={{
marginBottom: 20 }}>
```

```
                    <Text style={{
fontSize: 18
}}>{item.title}</Text>


<Text>{item.body}</Text>
                </View>
            ))}
        </View>
    );
}
```

Explanation:

- We're using fetch to request data from https://jsonplaceholder.typicode.com/post s, which is a free **API** that returns a list of posts.

- Inside useEffect, we fetch the data when the component mounts. We handle the response using .then(), parse it with .json(), and store the data in the state.

- If there is an error (e.g., no internet connection), it will be caught in the .catch() block, and we display an error message.

Using Axios

Axios is a promise-based library that makes HTTP requests easier. It's commonly used for its simplicity and rich feature set, including automatic JSON parsing, request cancellation, and more.

To get started with Axios, install it via npm:

bash

```
npm install axios
```

Here's an example of how to use Axios in React Native:

javascript

```
import React, { useState,
useEffect } from 'react';
import { View, Text,
ActivityIndicator } from 'react-
native';
import axios from 'axios';

const API_URL =
'https://jsonplaceholder.typicode.
com/posts';

export default function App() {
    const [data, setData] =
useState([]);
    const [loading, setLoading] =
useState(true);
    const [error, setError] =
useState(null);

    useEffect(() => {
```

```
    // Fetch data from the API
using Axios
        axios
            .get(API_URL)
            .then(response => {

setData(response.data); // Store
data in state
                setLoading(false);
// Set loading state to false
                })
            .catch(err => {
                setError(err); //
Set error state
                setLoading(false);
// Set loading state to false in
case of error
                });
    }, []);

    if (loading) {
```

```
    return <ActivityIndicator
size="large" color="#0000ff" />;
  }


  if (error) {
    return <Text>Error:
{error.message}</Text>;
  }


  return (
    <View style={{ padding: 20
}}>
      <Text style={{
fontSize: 20, marginBottom: 10
}}>Fetched Posts:</Text>
      {data.map(item => (
        <View
key={item.id} style={{
marginBottom: 20 }}>
```

```
                    <Text style={{
fontSize: 18
}}>{item.title}</Text>


<Text>{item.body}</Text>
                </View>
            ))}
        </View>
    );
}
```

Explanation:

- The structure of the code is very similar to the fetch example, but here we use axios.get() to fetch the data.

- Axios automatically parses the response data to JSON, so there's no need to call .json() as in the fetch example.

- The error handling is done through .catch(), just like fetch, and any issues during the request are stored in the error state.

Both fetch and Axios work similarly, but Axios provides more features out of the box, making it a popular choice for more complex applications.

---

2. Displaying Dynamic Data in Components

Now that you understand how to fetch data using fetch and Axios, the next step is to display the dynamic data inside your React Native components.

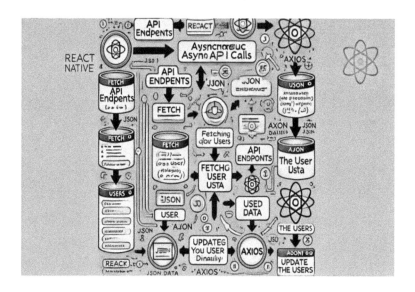

Displaying Fetched Data

React Native allows you to dynamically render components based on the data you fetch from an API. Let's break down how to display the data in your app.

Example of rendering dynamic data:

```javascript
import React, { useState,
useEffect } from 'react';
```

```
import { View, Text,
ActivityIndicator } from 'react-
native';
import axios from 'axios';

const API_URL =
'https://jsonplaceholder.typicode.
com/posts';

export default function App() {
    const [data, setData] =
useState([]);
    const [loading, setLoading] =
useState(true);
    const [error, setError] =
useState(null);

    useEffect(() => {
        // Fetch data using Axios
        axios.get(API_URL)
            .then(response => {
```

```
setData(response.data);
                setLoading(false);
        })
        .catch(err => {
            setError(err);
            setLoading(false);
        });
    }, []);

    if (loading) {
        return <ActivityIndicator
size="large" color="#0000ff" />;
    }

    if (error) {
        return <Text>Error:
{error.message}</Text>;
    }

    return (
```

```
      <View style={{ padding: 20
}}>
          <Text style={{
fontSize: 20, marginBottom: 10
}}>Fetched Posts:</Text>
          {data.map(item => (
              <View
key={item.id} style={{
marginBottom: 20 }}>
                  <Text style={{
fontSize: 18
}}>{item.title}</Text>

<Text>{item.body}</Text>
              </View>
          ))}
      </View>
   );
}
```

Explanation:

- We use the .map() method to loop through the array of posts in the data state and render them dynamically.

- For each item in the array, we display the title and body inside Text components.

- The use of key={item.id} ensures that each item has a unique identifier, which is important for React's internal optimization when rendering lists.

Rendering Nested Data

Sometimes, the data you fetch may be more complex, containing nested objects or arrays. In that case, you'll need to extract the required information and display it accordingly.

Example of rendering nested data:

```javascript

const nestedData = [
```

```
    { id: 1, user: { name:
'Alice', age: 25 }, post: { title:
'First Post', body: 'This is my
first post.' } },
    { id: 2, user: { name: 'Bob',
age: 30 }, post: { title: 'Second
Post', body: 'This is another
post.' } },
];


export default function App() {
    return (
        <View style={{ padding: 20
}}>
            {nestedData.map(item
=> (
                <View
key={item.id} style={{
marginBottom: 20 }}>
```

```
                    <Text style={{
fontSize: 18
}}>{item.user.name}</Text>


<Text>{item.user.age} years
old</Text>
                    <Text style={{
fontWeight: 'bold'
}}>{item.post.title}</Text>


<Text>{item.post.body}</Text>
              </View>
          ))}
        </View>
     );
}
```

Explanation:

- The nestedData array contains objects with both user and post objects nested inside each item.

- We extract the data for each user and post and render it accordingly in the UI.

---

3. Error Handling and Loading States

Handling loading states and errors is crucial when working with APIs. In the examples above, we've already used loading and error states, but let's dive deeper into best practices for managing these aspects.

Handling Loading States

When fetching data, you often need to show a loading indicator to inform the user that the app is waiting for the data. In React Native, we can use the ActivityIndicator component to display a loading spinner.

Here's an example of using ActivityIndicator:

```
javascript

import { ActivityIndicator } from
'react-native';

if (loading) {
    return <ActivityIndicator
size="large" color="#0000ff" />;
}
```

You can customize the size and color props to match your app's design. It's a good idea to show a loading spinner until the data has been successfully fetched.

Handling Errors Gracefully

Whenever you fetch data from an API, there's always a chance something could go wrong—whether it's a network issue or a problem with the API itself. It's important to handle errors and show meaningful messages to the user.

Here's how to display an error message:

javascript

```
if (error) {
    return <Text>Error:
{error.message}</Text>;
}
```

You can customize the error message depending on the type of error. For example, if the error is related to network issues, you can display a message like "Please check your internet connection."

Timeouts and Retry Logic

Sometimes APIs might take longer to respond than expected. In such cases, you can implement a timeout to avoid waiting indefinitely for a response.

Example of handling a timeout:

```javascript
const fetchDataWithTimeout = async
() => {
    try {
        const response = await
axios.get(API_URL, { timeout: 5000
});
        setData(response.data);
    } catch (error) {
        if (error.code ===
'ECONNABORTED') {
            setError('Request
timed out');
        } else {

setError(error.message);
        }
    }
};
```

This example sets a 5-second timeout for the API request and handles errors accordingly.

Conclusion

In this chapter, we explored the essential concepts of working with APIs in React Native. We covered the basics of fetching data using both fetch and Axios, displaying dynamic data in components, and handling loading and error states gracefully.

By mastering these techniques, you can build dynamic apps that fetch data from remote APIs and present it in a user-friendly way. As you build more complex apps, you can refine your error handling and implement features like retry logic and data caching.

In the next chapter, we'll explore **State Management** and **Global State** in React Native, where you'll learn how to manage state across different components and screens efficiently. Keep experimenting with APIs and remember: handling data is the backbone of any interactive app!

Chapter 8: Handling User Input in React Native

Introduction

User input is a core feature of many mobile applications. Whether it's gathering user data through forms, handling text input for a search bar, or validating user input for accuracy, managing input is an essential part of app development. React Native provides several components, including **TextInput** and **Forms**, to help you collect, process, and validate user input.

In this chapter, we will walk through:

- Using **Forms** and **TextInput** components to capture user input.

- Validating user input to ensure that the data entered is correct and meets the required criteria.

- Handling **keyboard** and **scroll** behaviors to create a smooth user experience, especially on mobile devices.

By the end of this chapter, you will have a strong understanding of how to handle user input in your React Native apps, empowering you to create interactive, user-friendly applications.

1. Forms and TextInput Components

The **TextInput** component is the most commonly used form element in React Native for collecting user input. It allows users to type in a field, and React Native provides various props to customize the behavior and appearance of the TextInput component.

Basic Usage of TextInput

Let's begin by exploring how to use the **TextInput** component in its simplest form. Here's a basic example where we capture a user's name:

```jsx
import React, { useState } from 'react';
```

```
import { View, TextInput, Text,
StyleSheet } from 'react-native';

export default function App() {
    const [name, setName] =
useState('');

    return (
        <View
style={styles.container}>
            <TextInput

style={styles.input}
                placeholder="Enter
your name"

onChangeText={(text) =>
setName(text)}  // Updates state
with the input value
                value={name}  //
Binds the input field to the state
```

```
            />
            <Text>Hello,
{name}!</Text>
        </View>
    );
}


const styles = StyleSheet.create({
    container: {
        flex: 1,
        justifyContent: 'center',
        alignItems: 'center',
    },
    input: {
        height: 40,
        borderColor: 'gray',
        borderWidth: 1,
        marginBottom: 20,
        paddingLeft: 10,
        width: '80%',
    },
```

```
});
```

Explanation:

- The **TextInput** component captures user input for the name.

- The onChangeText prop is used to update the component's state whenever the user types something.

- The value prop binds the input field to the state, ensuring that the displayed text stays in sync with the state.

Handling Multiple Inputs in a Form

In many cases, you may have a form with multiple TextInput fields. Here's an example of a simple form with a name and email field:

```jsx
import React, { useState } from 'react';
```

```
import { View, TextInput, Button,
Text, StyleSheet } from 'react-
native';

export default function App() {
    const [name, setName] =
useState('');
    const [email, setEmail] =
useState('');
    const [message, setMessage] =
useState('');

    const handleSubmit = () => {
        // Handle form submission
(e.g., send data to an API or save
to local storage)
        setMessage(`Hello ${name},
we have received your email:
${email}`);
    };
```

```
    return (
        <View
style={styles.container}>
            <TextInput

style={styles.input}
                placeholder="Enter
your name"

onChangeText={setName}  //
Directly updating state with the
input
                value={name}
            />
            <TextInput

style={styles.input}
                placeholder="Enter
your email"

onChangeText={setEmail}
```

```
            value={email}
      />
      <Button title="Submit"
onPress={handleSubmit} />
      {message &&
<Text>{message}</Text>} {/*
Display confirmation message */}
      </View>
  );
}


const styles = StyleSheet.create({
  container: {
    flex: 1,
    justifyContent: 'center',
    alignItems: 'center',
    padding: 20,
  },
  input: {
    height: 40,
    borderColor: 'gray',
```

```
    borderWidth: 1,
    marginBottom: 10,
    paddingLeft: 10,
    width: '80%',
  },
});
```

Explanation:

- We use multiple TextInput components to capture different pieces of information from the user.

- The state for each TextInput is managed individually (name, email).

- When the form is submitted, the handleSubmit function runs, and the form data is displayed.

2. Validating User Input

It's crucial to validate user input before using it in your app, whether you're submitting it to a backend server or storing it locally. Validation ensures that the data entered by users is correct and in the expected format.

Basic Validation

Here's an example of validating a user's email address:

```jsx
import React, { useState } from
'react';
import { View, TextInput, Button,
Text, StyleSheet } from 'react-
native';

export default function App() {
```

```
    const [email, setEmail] =
useState('');
    const [error, setError] =
useState('');

    const validateEmail = (email)
=> {
        const regex =
/\S+@\S+\.\S+/;
        return regex.test(email);
    };

    const handleSubmit = () => {
        if (!validateEmail(email))
{
            setError('Please enter
a valid email address.');
        } else {
            setError('');
            // Proceed with the
form submission
```

```
        alert('Email is
valid!');
        }
    };

    return (
        <View
style={styles.container}>
            <TextInput

style={styles.input}
            placeholder="Enter
your email"

onChangeText={setEmail}
            value={email}
        />
        {error && <Text
style={styles.errorText}>{error}</
Text>}
```

```
      <Button title="Submit"
onPress={handleSubmit} />
      </View>
   );
}


const styles = StyleSheet.create({
   container: {
      flex: 1,
      justifyContent: 'center',
      alignItems: 'center',
      padding: 20,
   },
   input: {
      height: 40,
      borderColor: 'gray',
      borderWidth: 1,
      marginBottom: 10,
      paddingLeft: 10,
      width: '80%',
   },
```

```
errorText: {
    color: 'red',
    marginBottom: 10,
},
});
```

Explanation:

- The validateEmail function checks if the email follows a proper format using a regular expression (regex).

- If the email is invalid, an error message is displayed; otherwise, the form proceeds.

Advanced Validation with Multiple Fields

In real-world scenarios, you may need to validate multiple fields at once. For example, validating both a password and confirm password field:

```jsx

import React, { useState } from 'react';
import { View, TextInput, Button, Text, StyleSheet } from 'react-native';

export default function App() {
    const [password, setPassword] = useState('');
    const [confirmPassword, setConfirmPassword] = useState('');
    const [error, setError] = useState('');

    const validateForm = () => {
        if (password !== confirmPassword) {
```

```
        setError('Passwords do
not match!');
      } else {
        setError('');
        alert('Form submitted
successfully!');
      }
    };


    return (
      <View
style={styles.container}>
        <TextInput

style={styles.input}
          placeholder="Enter
your password"
          secureTextEntry

onChangeText={setPassword}
          value={password}
```

```
            />
            <TextInput

style={styles.input}

placeholder="Confirm your
password"
                    secureTextEntry

onChangeText={setConfirmPassword}

value={confirmPassword}
            />
            {error && <Text
style={styles.errorText}>{error}</
Text>}
            <Button title="Submit"
onPress={validateForm} />
        </View>
    );
}
```

```
const styles = StyleSheet.create({
    container: {
        flex: 1,
        justifyContent: 'center',
        alignItems: 'center',
        padding: 20,
    },
    input: {
        height: 40,
        borderColor: 'gray',
        borderWidth: 1,
        marginBottom: 10,
        paddingLeft: 10,
        width: '80%',
    },
    errorText: {
        color: 'red',
        marginBottom: 10,
    },
});
```

Explanation:

- We added validation for password confirmation to ensure that both the password and confirmPassword fields match.

- If they don't match, an error message is displayed.

---

3. Handling Keyboard and Scroll Behaviors

On mobile devices, managing the keyboard is an important part of creating a smooth user experience. When users type into a TextInput, the keyboard may cover parts of the screen. React Native offers several ways to handle this behavior, such as using the **KeyboardAvoidingView** and **ScrollView** components.

Using KeyboardAvoidingView

KeyboardAvoidingView is a React Native component that automatically adjusts the position of input fields when the keyboard appears, preventing the keyboard from covering the fields.

```jsx

import React, { useState } from 'react';
import { View, TextInput, Button, StyleSheet, KeyboardAvoidingView, Platform } from 'react-native';
```

```
export default function App() {
    const [email, setEmail] =
useState('');

    return (
        <KeyboardAvoidingView

style={styles.container}
            behavior={Platform.OS
=== 'ios' ? 'padding' : 'height'}
        >
            <TextInput

style={styles.input}
                placeholder="Enter
your email"

onChangeText={setEmail}
                value={email}
            />
```

```
        <Button title="Submit"
onPress={() => alert('Form
submitted!')} />
        </KeyboardAvoidingView>
    );
}


const styles = StyleSheet.create({
    container: {
        flex: 1,
        justifyContent: 'center',
        alignItems: 'center',
        padding: 20,
    },
    input: {
        height: 40,
        borderColor: 'gray',
        borderWidth: 1,
        marginBottom: 10,
        paddingLeft: 10,
        width: '80%',
```

```
    },
});
```

Explanation:

- The KeyboardAvoidingView component is wrapped around the input fields and button, ensuring that when the keyboard appears, it adjusts the layout accordingly.

- We use the behavior prop to specify how the view should behave when the keyboard appears ('padding' for iOS and 'height' for Android).

Using ScrollView for Larger Forms

If your form is large, you may want to make the entire form scrollable so users can scroll through the fields without being blocked by the keyboard. Here's how to use **ScrollView** in conjunction with KeyboardAvoidingView:

```jsx
```

```
import React, { useState } from
'react';
import { ScrollView, TextInput,
Button, StyleSheet,
KeyboardAvoidingView, Platform }
from 'react-native';

export default function App() {
    const [email, setEmail] =
useState('');

    return (
        <KeyboardAvoidingView

style={styles.container}
            behavior={Platform.OS
=== 'ios' ? 'padding' : 'height'}
        >
```

```
        <ScrollView
contentContainerStyle={styles.scro
llContainer}>
                <TextInput

style={styles.input}

placeholder="Enter your email"

onChangeText={setEmail}
                    value={email}
            />
                <Button
title="Submit" onPress={() =>
alert('Form submitted!')} />
            </ScrollView>
        </KeyboardAvoidingView>
    );
}

const styles = StyleSheet.create({
```

```
container: {
    flex: 1,
},
scrollContainer: {
    flexGrow: 1,
    justifyContent: 'center',
    alignItems: 'center',
},
input: {
    height: 40,
    borderColor: 'gray',
    borderWidth: 1,
    marginBottom: 10,
    paddingLeft: 10,
    width: '80%',
},
});
```

Explanation:

- **ScrollView** is used to make the form scrollable. The contentContainerStyle ensures the content is centered.

- This is especially useful for larger forms with many fields, as it allows the user to scroll through the form without the keyboard covering up any fields.

Conclusion

In this chapter, we've covered how to handle user input in React Native. You learned how to:

- Use **TextInput** components to capture user input in forms.

- Validate user input, ensuring that it's correct before submission.

- Handle **keyboard behavior** and **scrolling** to improve the user experience, especially when dealing with forms.

By applying these techniques, you can create responsive and user-friendly forms in your React Native apps. With proper validation and smooth keyboard handling, you will ensure that your users have a seamless experience while interacting with your app.

In the next chapter, we will delve into **State Management** and how to handle app-wide state using React Native's built-in tools or third-party libraries.

Chapter 9: State Management in React Native

Introduction

State management is one of the most important aspects of app development, especially in React Native, where data changes frequently in response to user interactions. React, by default, provides a **state** feature that allows components to maintain and update data. However, as applications grow in size and complexity, managing state locally within individual components becomes increasingly difficult.

In this chapter, we will dive deep into the concept of **state management** in React Native. You will learn:

- How **React's state** and **Context API** work for managing local and global state.

- An **introduction to Redux**, a powerful library used for state management in larger apps.

- How to manage **app state globally** in React Native applications, ensuring smooth data flow across different components.

This chapter is designed for all skill levels, with plenty of practical examples to help you understand and implement state management in your own React Native applications.

---

1. Understanding React's State and Context API

State management is crucial for creating dynamic, interactive apps. React's **state** is an object that determines how a component renders and behaves. It stores data that can change over time, such as user input, responses from APIs, or the status of a button (enabled/disabled).

React State Basics

Each component in React can have its own local state. The useState hook is used to define state variables and functions for updating them. For example:

```
jsx
```

```
import React, { useState } from
'react';
import { View, Text, Button } from
'react-native';

export default function Counter()
{
    const [count, setCount] =
useState(0); // Declare state
variable `count`

    return (
        <View>
            <Text>Count:
{count}</Text>
            <Button
title="Increment" onPress={() =>
setCount(count + 1)} />
        </View>
    );
```

}

Explanation:

- **useState(0)** initializes the state variable count with a value of 0.

- **setCount()** is the function that updates the state variable whenever the button is pressed.

- This allows React to re-render the component whenever the state changes.

When to Use Local State

Local state is great for managing small, component-specific data, like form inputs or toggle states. However, as your app grows, it may become more complex, requiring a way to manage state across multiple components or even globally within the entire app.

Context API: A Step Toward Global State

To manage state across multiple components without passing props down through every level, React provides the **Context API**. Context allows you to share data at different levels of your component tree without explicitly passing props.

Here's how to set up and use the Context API:

1. **Create Context:**

jsx

```
import React, { createContext,
useState } from 'react';


// Create a Context object
export const AppContext =
createContext();
```

2. **Provide Context to Components:**

jsx

```
export default function App() {
```

```jsx
    const [theme, setTheme] =
useState('light');


    return (
        <AppContext.Provider
value={{ theme, setTheme }}>
            <HomeScreen />
        </AppContext.Provider>
    );
}
```

3. **Consume Context in a Component:**

jsx

```jsx
import React, { useContext } from
'react';
import { Text, Button, View } from
'react-native';
import { AppContext } from
'./App';
```

```
export default function
HomeScreen() {
    const { theme, setTheme } =
useContext(AppContext); // Access
context

    return (
        <View>
            <Text>The current
theme is {theme}</Text>
            <Button
                title="Toggle
Theme"
                onPress={() =>
setTheme(theme === 'light' ?
'dark' : 'light')}
            />
        </View>
    );
}
```

Explanation:

- **AppContext** is created to store the theme state and the setTheme function.

- The AppContext.Provider wraps the HomeScreen component and provides the state to its children.

- Inside HomeScreen, we use the useContext hook to access the theme and setTheme.

This approach allows you to easily manage and share state across your app, but it still has limitations when the app grows larger.

---

2. Introduction to Redux for State Management

When an app becomes complex and needs to share state across many components, the Context API may not be sufficient. This is where **Redux** comes in. Redux is a predictable state container for JavaScript apps that helps manage state globally. It is commonly used in large-scale React applications due to its scalability and flexibility.

What Is Redux?

Redux works by maintaining the **global state** in a central store. Components can **dispatch actions** to update the state, and the state changes are handled by **reducers.**

1. **Store:** Holds the state of the app.

2. **Actions:** Plain JavaScript objects that describe what happened.

3. **Reducers:** Functions that specify how the state changes in response to actions.

Setting Up Redux

To get started with Redux, you need to install the necessary dependencies:

```bash
npm install redux react-redux
```

1. Creating Actions

Actions are plain JavaScript objects that represent an intention to change the state.

```jsx
// actions.js
export const increment = () => {
    return {
        type: 'INCREMENT',
    };
};
```

2. Creating Reducers

Reducers specify how the app's state changes in response to an action.

```jsx
```

```
// reducer.js
const initialState = {
    count: 0,
};

const counterReducer = (state =
initialState, action) => {
    switch (action.type) {
        case 'INCREMENT':
            return { count:
state.count + 1 };
        default:
            return state;
    }
};

export default counterReducer;
```

3. Creating the Store

The store brings together the actions and reducers and manages the app's state.

```jsx
// store.js
import { createStore } from
'redux';
import counterReducer from
'./reducer';

const store =
createStore(counterReducer);

export default store;
```

4. Connecting Redux with React Components

Now, we need to connect Redux to our React Native app using **React-Redux**.

```jsx
import React from 'react';
```

```
import { View, Text, Button } from
'react-native';
import { connect } from 'react-
redux';
import { increment } from
'./actions';

function App({ count, increment })
{
    return (
        <View>
            <Text>Count:
{count}</Text>
            <Button
title="Increment"
onPress={increment} />
        </View>
    );
}
```

```
const mapStateToProps = (state) =>
{
    return { count: state.count };
};


export default
connect(mapStateToProps, {
increment })(App);
```

Explanation:

- We use connect from react-redux to connect the Redux state (mapStateToProps) and the action (increment) to the component.

- The count value is retrieved from the global store and displayed in the component.

- The increment action is dispatched when the button is pressed, and the Redux state is updated.

Why Redux?

Redux provides a single source of truth for your app's state, which makes debugging easier, especially with the **Redux DevTools**. It also ensures that state updates are predictable and follow a strict pattern, making it more scalable and maintainable for large applications.

---

3. Managing App State Globally

As your app grows in complexity, managing state globally across different screens or components becomes essential. Redux allows you to manage the app's state in a global store and ensures that data can be accessed or updated by any component in the app.

Working with Async Data in Redux

In real-world apps, your state will often need to interact with asynchronous data, such as fetching from an API. Redux allows you to handle async data through **middleware** like **redux-thunk** or **redux-saga**.

Using Redux-Thunk for Async Actions

To install redux-thunk, run:

```bash
```

```bash
npm install redux-thunk
```

Then, set up redux-thunk in your Redux store:

```jsx
```

```jsx
import { createStore,
applyMiddleware } from 'redux';
import thunk from 'redux-thunk';
import counterReducer from
'./reducer';

const store =
createStore(counterReducer,
applyMiddleware(thunk));
```

Next, create an async action that
fetches data from an API:
jsx

```
// actions.js
export const fetchData = () => {
    return (dispatch) => {
        dispatch({ type:
'FETCH_DATA_REQUEST' });

fetch('https://jsonplaceholder.typ
icode.com/posts')
```

```
        .then((response) =>
response.json())
        .then((data) => {
            dispatch({ type:
'FETCH_DATA_SUCCESS', payload:
data });
        })
        .catch((error) => {
            dispatch({ type:
'FETCH_DATA_FAILURE', error });
        });
    };
};
```

Handling the Async Actions in Reducers

Modify the reducer to handle async actions:

jsx

```
const initialState = {
    data: [],
```

```
    loading: false,
    error: null,
};


const dataReducer = (state =
initialState, action) => {
    switch (action.type) {
        case 'FETCH_DATA_REQUEST':
            return { ...state,
loading: true };
        case 'FETCH_DATA_SUCCESS':
            return { ...state,
loading: false, data:
action.payload };
        case 'FETCH_DATA_FAILURE':
            return { ...state,
loading: false, error:
action.error };
        default:
            return state;
    }
```

```
};
```

```
export default dataReducer;
```

Displaying Async Data in Components

Now that the state has been updated, you can display the fetched data in your component:

```jsx
jsx
```

```jsx
import React, { useEffect } from
'react';
import { View, Text,
ActivityIndicator } from 'react-
native';
import { connect } from 'react-
redux';
import { fetchData } from
'./actions';
```

```
function DataScreen({ data,
loading, error, fetchData }) {
    useEffect(() => {
        fetchData();
    }, [fetchData]);

    if (loading) {
        return <ActivityIndicator
size="large" color="#0000ff" />;
    }

    if (error) {
        return <Text>Error:
{error.message}</Text>;
    }

    return (
        <View>
            {data.map((item) => (
                <Text
key={item.id}>{item.title}</Text>
```

```
        )))}
      </View>
    );
}


const mapStateToProps = (state) =>
{
    return { data: state.data,
loading: state.loading, error:
state.error };
};


export default
connect(mapStateToProps, {
fetchData })(DataScreen);
```

Explanation:

- We use **redux-thunk** to handle the asynchronous API request inside the action.

- The component dispatches the fetchData action, which updates the state with the fetched data, and then renders the results.

Conclusion

State management is a crucial aspect of React Native app development. In this chapter, we've covered the basics of managing state using React's useState hook, the **Context API** for managing global state, and **Redux** for more complex state management in larger apps.

We also explored how to manage async data with **redux-thunk**, which allows you to handle side-effects like **API** calls and manage them inside Redux.

By understanding and implementing state management effectively, you can create more scalable, maintainable, and predictable React

Native applications. In the next chapter, we'll dive into **Advanced UI Components** and how to leverage React Native's powerful components to create visually appealing user interfaces.

Keep experimenting with state management, and remember: the right state management strategy can make your app more robust, efficient, and easier to maintain!

Chapter 10: Debugging and Testing in React Native

Introduction

Debugging and testing are integral parts of software development, helping ensure your app functions as intended and performs reliably under various conditions. In React Native development, debugging and testing can seem daunting due to the variety of tools and techniques available. However, understanding the right tools and methods can significantly streamline your development process, making your apps more robust and error-free.

In this chapter, we will explore the following topics:

1. **Setting up debugging tools**, including **React Native Debugger** and **Chrome Developer Tools**, to help identify and fix issues in your app.

2. **Writing unit and integration tests** using Jest, ensuring that your components and functions are working correctly.

3. **Handling errors and warnings effectively**, so that you can proactively deal with issues before they affect your app's users.

This chapter is designed to be both practical and accessible, with examples and step-by-step instructions to guide you through the debugging and testing process.

1. Setting Up Debugging Tools

Debugging is an essential skill for any developer. React Native provides several tools to make this process easier, and we'll focus on the two most widely used: **React Native Debugger** and **Chrome Developer Tools**.

Using React Native Debugger

React Native Debugger is an all-in-one debugging tool that integrates with Redux and the React Native Inspector. It provides you with a UI to inspect elements, view the state, and track network requests, making it an essential tool for debugging React Native apps.

Setting Up React Native Debugger

1. Install React Native Debugger:

*For **macOS**, **Windows**, and **Linux**, you can install React Native Debugger using the following command:*
bash

brew update && brew cask install react-native-debugger

If you are not using **Homebrew**, you can download the application directly from GitHub releases.

2. Launch React Native Debugger:

- o After installing, run the debugger by typing:

bash

open -a "React Native Debugger"

3. **Connect React Native Debugger to your app:**

- First, start your app in the development mode by running:

```bash
```

```bash
react-native run-android
```
or

```bash
```

```bash
react-native run-ios
```

- Once your app is running, open the in-app developer menu by shaking your device or using the keyboard shortcut Cmd+D for iOS or Cmd+M for Android.

- Select **Debug** from the menu to open the **JavaScript Debugger** in your browser.

○ The React Native Debugger should now automatically connect and start inspecting your app.

Features of React Native Debugger

- **Network Requests**: View all network requests your app makes and inspect their responses, status codes, headers, and payload.

- **Redux Integration**: If your app uses Redux, React Native Debugger shows actions, state changes, and allows you to inspect the store.

- **JavaScript Console**: You can log errors and use the console to run JavaScript code in the context of your app.

- **React Component Inspector**: Inspect React components, view their state and props, and explore the component tree.

Using Chrome Developer Tools

Chrome Developer Tools (DevTools) are built-in tools for inspecting and debugging JavaScript applications. React Native uses Chrome DevTools for debugging JavaScript code.

Setting Up Chrome Developer Tools

1. **Enable Debugging**:

   o Start your app using react-native run-android or react-native run-ios.

   o Open the developer menu (shake your device or use Cmd+D or Cmd+M).

   o Select **Debug** to enable debugging in Chrome.

- o A new Chrome tab should open automatically, with the JavaScript console available.

2. **Using DevTools**:

- o You can now use the **Console, Elements Inspector,** and **Network** tabs to debug your app.

- o The **Console** tab shows logs, errors, and warnings.

- o The **Network** tab lets you inspect network requests.

Using Console Logs for Debugging

While debugging, console.log() is one of the most useful tools at your disposal. Use it to print out values, check variable states, or track function executions. For example:

javascript

```
console.log('App started');

console.log('User data:', userData);
```

These log statements will appear in the Chrome DevTools console, helping you trace the flow of your app and pinpoint issues.

---

2. Writing Unit and Integration Tests with Jest

Testing ensures that your app functions as expected and helps catch bugs before they reach production. In React Native, **Jest** is the default testing framework, making it simple to write unit and integration tests for your components and functions.

Setting Up Jest

Jest is already included with React Native, so you don't need to install it manually. To run Jest tests, make sure you have the following dependencies in your package.json:

json

```json
"devDependencies": {
    "jest": "^26.0.1",
    "react-test-renderer": "17.0.1"
}
```

Running Tests

To run Jest tests, use the following command:

bash

```bash
npm test
```

This command runs all test files with the .test.js or .spec.js extension.

Writing Unit Tests

Unit tests focus on testing individual functions or components. Let's write a simple unit test for a function that adds two numbers:

javascript

```javascript
// add.js
export function add(a, b) {
    return a + b;
}
```

Now, write a test for this function:

javascript

```javascript
// add.test.js
import { add } from './add';

test('adds 1 + 2 to equal 3', ()
=> {
    expect(add(1, 2)).toBe(3);
});
```

Explanation:

- **test()** is a Jest function that defines a test case.

- **expect()** is used to assert the expected value.

- **toBe()** is a matcher function that checks if the result matches the expected value.

Writing Component Tests

Now, let's write a test for a React Native component. Suppose we have the following Button component:

javascript

```
// Button.js
import React from 'react';
import { Button as RNButton } from
'react-native';
```

```
export function Button({ onPress,
title }) {
    return <RNButton
onPress={onPress} title={title}
/>;
}
```

We can test this component with Jest and the **react-test-renderer** library.

```javascript
// Button.test.js
import React from 'react';
import { render } from '@testing-library/react-native';
import { Button } from './Button';

test('Button renders correctly', () => {
    const { getByText } =
render(<Button title="Click me" />);
```

```
    const button =
getByText('Click me');
    expect(button).toBeTruthy();
});
```

Explanation:

- **render()** from **@testing-library/react-native** is used to render the component.

- **getByText()** is used to find the button by its text label.

- **toBeTruthy()** asserts that the button is rendered successfully.

Integration Tests

Integration tests check how multiple parts of the application work together. Let's test a form that uses a button and a text input. The form should display the entered text when the button is pressed.

javascript

```
// Form.js
import React, { useState } from
'react';
import { TextInput, Button, Text,
View } from 'react-native';

export function Form() {
    const [text, setText] =
useState('');

    const handlePress = () => {
        setText('Hello, ' + text);
    };

    return (
        <View>
            <TextInput
value={text}
onChangeText={setText} />
```

```
        <Button title="Submit"
onPress={handlePress} />
        <Text>{text}</Text>
      </View>
    );
}
```

We can write an integration test for this form:

javascript

```
// Form.test.js
import React from 'react';
import { render, fireEvent } from
'@testing-library/react-native';
import { Form } from './Form';

test('displays the entered text
after submit', () => {
    const { getByText, getByRole }
= render(<Form />);
```

```
    const input =
getByRole('textinput');
    fireEvent.changeText(input,
'John');

    const button =
getByText('Submit');
    fireEvent.press(button);

    expect(getByText('Hello,
John')).toBeTruthy();
});
```

Explanation:

- **fireEvent.changeText()** simulates typing into the TextInput.

- **fireEvent.press()** simulates pressing the submit button.

- **getByText()** verifies if the text has been updated after the button press.

3. Handling Errors and Warnings Effectively

When developing mobile apps, you will inevitably encounter errors and warnings. Handling them properly ensures a better user experience and helps maintain a clean and efficient codebase.

Common Errors and Warnings in React Native

React Native provides several warnings that help catch potential issues during development. For example:

- **Invalid Prop Type Warnings**: React will warn you if a component receives a prop of the wrong type.

- **Deprecation Warnings**: React Native occasionally deprecates certain APIs, and you may receive warnings if you're using them.

Handling Console Errors

For debugging, use **console.log()**, **console.warn()**, and **console.error()** to log different types of messages.

Example of logging errors:

```javascript

try {
    throw new Error('Something
went wrong');
} catch (error) {
    console.error('Caught error:',
error.message);
}
```

You can use **console.error()** for critical errors and **console.warn()** for warnings.

Suppressing Warnings in Production

You might want to suppress certain warnings or log statements in production. This can be done by using the following snippet:

```javascript

if (__DEV__) {
```

```
console.log('This log will
only appear in development');
}
```

__DEV__ is a special global variable that checks whether the app is in development mode.

Using Error Boundaries for Component-Level Error Handling

In React, you can use **Error Boundaries** to catch JavaScript errors anywhere in a component tree and display a fallback UI instead of crashing the component.

Example:

```javascript


import React, { Component } from
'react';
import { Text, View } from 'react-
native';
```

```
class ErrorBoundary extends
Component {
    state = { hasError: false };

    static
getDerivedStateFromError(error) {
        return { hasError: true };
    }

    componentDidCatch(error, info)
{
        console.error(error,
info);
    }

    render() {
        if (this.state.hasError) {
            return <Text>Something
went wrong.</Text>;
        }
```

```
        return
this.props.children;
    }
}


export default function App() {
    return (
        <ErrorBoundary>
            <SomeComponent />
        </ErrorBoundary>
    );
}
```

Explanation:

- **getDerivedStateFromError()** updates the state to indicate an error has occurred.

- **componentDidCatch()** logs the error and additional info for debugging.

- The app renders a fallback UI when an error is caught.

Conclusion

In this chapter, we explored essential tools and techniques for **debugging and testing** React Native applications:

- **React Native Debugger** and **Chrome Developer Tools** for efficient debugging.

- **Jest** for writing unit and integration tests that help verify your app's functionality.

- **Error boundaries** and effective error handling practices to ensure smooth user experiences.

By mastering these debugging and testing techniques, you can improve your app's reliability, reduce errors, and ensure a seamless development process. In the next chapter, we will dive into **Performance Optimization** to ensure your app runs efficiently and smoothly across different devices.

Happy coding, and remember: debugging and testing are not just tasks but integral parts of building high-quality, maintainable applications!

Chapter 11: Performance Optimization in React Native

Introduction

As mobile applications become more complex, ensuring they perform efficiently becomes a critical task. A slow app can lead to frustrated users, poor app reviews, and ultimately, a failed product. React Native is an excellent framework for building cross-platform mobile apps, but just like any framework, it requires thoughtful attention to performance, especially as your app scales. In this chapter, we'll explore several performance optimization strategies for React Native, helping you ensure that your app runs smoothly on both iOS and Android devices.

In this chapter, we'll cover:

- **Profiling and improving app performance**: How to measure and optimize your app's performance.

- **Lazy loading components and optimizing re-renders**: Reducing the load time of your app and improving rendering performance.

- **Using native modules for performance-critical tasks**: When and how to offload performance-heavy tasks to native code.

By the end of this chapter, you'll have the knowledge to make your React Native app run faster, more smoothly, and more efficiently.

1. Profiling and Improving App Performance

To improve performance, you first need to understand where your app's performance bottlenecks lie. Profiling tools can help you identify slow parts of your app, so you can target them for optimization.

Using the React Native Performance Monitor

React Native has a built-in performance monitor that you can use to profile your app and check various performance metrics. This monitor provides insights into the CPU, memory, and network usage of your app.

How to Enable the Performance Monitor

1. Start your app by running it in development mode with react-native run-android or react-native run-ios.

2. Open the **developer menu** (shake your device or use Cmd+D on iOS or Cmd+M on Android).

3. Select **"Enable Performance Monitor"** to start viewing performance metrics.

The performance monitor will show you the following metrics:

- **FPS (Frames Per Second)**: The number of frames your app renders per second. A smooth app should maintain at least 60 FPS.

- **JS Thread**: The JavaScript thread is responsible for handling all the logic in your app. It's important to keep this thread as unburdened as possible for smooth performance.

- **UI Thread**: The UI thread handles rendering the app's user interface. High activity on the UI thread can cause janky animations and slowdowns.

Using the Chrome Developer Tools for Profiling

You can also use **Chrome DevTools** to profile your React Native app. Here's how to use them:

1. Start your app in debug mode (react-native run-android or react-native run-ios).

2. Open the **developer menu** and choose **"Debug"** to open the app in Chrome.

3. Open **Chrome DevTools** by navigating to chrome://inspect and selecting your app.

4. In Chrome DevTools, you can use the **Performance tab** to record and analyze JavaScript execution.

By recording the performance, you can see where bottlenecks are occurring and optimize the parts of your app that are taking too long to execute.

Optimizing CPU Usage

If your app is running slowly due to high CPU usage, consider the following strategies:

- **Debounce or throttle events**: For actions like scrolling, button presses, or input field changes, use **debouncing** or **throttling** to limit how often the event triggers the app's logic.

- **Offload heavy calculations**: Move intensive computations to native code or offload them to background threads where possible.

Example: Throttling a Scroll Event

```javascript
import React, { useState } from
'react';
import { ScrollView, Text, View }
from 'react-native';
import { useDebouncedCallback }
from 'use-debounce';

export default function App() {
    const [scrollPosition,
setScrollPosition] = useState(0);

    const handleScroll =
useDebouncedCallback((e) => {
```

```
setScrollPosition(e.nativeEvent.co
ntentOffset.y);
    }, 100); // Debounced by 100ms
to avoid frequent updates

    return (
        <ScrollView
onScroll={handleScroll}>
            <Text>{`Scroll
position:
${scrollPosition}`}</Text>
            {/* Additional content
here */}
        </ScrollView>
    );
}
```

Optimizing Memory Usage

Memory leaks can drastically affect performance, especially in apps with large datasets. You can optimize memory usage by:

- Using **flat lists** instead of regular lists or arrays, as they are optimized for rendering large lists with minimal memory.

- Avoiding unnecessary re-renders or holding large objects in memory.

---

2. Lazy Loading Components and Optimizing Re-renders

One of the most important performance optimizations in React Native is reducing unnecessary re-renders. React components re-render whenever their state or props change, but this can be costly in terms of performance, especially for large applications.

Using React.memo to Prevent Unnecessary Re-renders

React.memo is a higher-order component that helps you prevent unnecessary re-renders for functional components. It ensures that the component only re-renders when its props change.

Example of Using React.memo

javascript

```
import React from 'react';
```

```
import { View, Text } from 'react-
native';

const ListItem = React.memo(({
item }) => {
    console.log('Rendering:',
item.name);
    return (
        <View>

<Text>{item.name}</Text>
        </View>
    );
});

export default function App() {
    const items = [{ name: 'Item
1' }, { name: 'Item 2' }];
    return (
        <View>
```

```
        {items.map((item,
index) => (
            <ListItem
key={index} item={item} />
        ))}
    </View>
  );
}
```

Explanation:

- React.memo prevents re-renders of ListItem if the item prop remains the same between renders. This is particularly useful for list components or components that are used repeatedly.

Lazy Loading Components

For large applications, you may not need all components to load at once. **Lazy loading** is a technique where components are loaded only when they are needed.

React Native provides the React.lazy() function, which works with dynamic import() to load components only when they are required.

Example of Lazy Loading a Component

```javascript

import React, { Suspense, lazy }
from 'react';
import { View, Text } from 'react-native';

const LazyComponent = lazy(() =>
import('./LazyComponent'));

export default function App() {
    return (
        <View>
            <Text>Welcome to the
app!</Text>
```

```
      <Suspense
fallback={<Text>Loading...</Text>}
>
            <LazyComponent />
      </Suspense>
    </View>
  );
}
```

Explanation:

- React.lazy() dynamically imports the LazyComponent only when it is needed.

- The Suspense component is used to show a loading indicator until the component is fully loaded.

Optimizing Re-renders with useCallback

In some cases, functions passed as props can cause unnecessary re-renders. The useCallback hook helps optimize this by memoizing functions so that they are not recreated on every render.

Example of Using useCallback

```javascript
import React, { useState,
useCallback } from 'react';
import { Button, View } from
'react-native';

export default function App() {
    const [count, setCount] =
useState(0);

    const increment =
useCallback(() => {
        setCount(count + 1);
    }, [count]);

    return (
```

```
    <View>
        <Button
title="Increment"
onPress={increment} />
        <Text>Count:
{count}</Text>
    </View>
  );
}
```

Explanation:

- useCallback ensures that the increment function is not recreated unless count changes, reducing unnecessary re-renders of components that depend on it.

---

3. Using Native Modules for Performance-Critical Tasks

In some cases, JavaScript may not provide the necessary performance for computationally intensive tasks, such as image processing or heavy calculations. In these cases, **native modules** allow you to offload the task to native code (written in Java, Objective-C, or Swift) for better performance.

When to Use Native Modules

- **CPU-Intensive Operations**: Complex mathematical calculations, data processing, etc.

- **Heavy File I/O**: Reading and writing large files from the filesystem.

- **Graphics-Intensive Tasks**: Image or video processing.

- **Low-Level Access**: Access to hardware like Bluetooth, sensors, or camera functionalities.

Creating a Native Module

1. **Creating the Native Module**: In iOS, you write a native module in Objective-C or Swift. In Android, you write it in Java.

2. **Example: Image Processing in a Native Module (iOS)**

First, create a new **Objective-C** file (e.g., ImageProcessor.m):

```objc

#import <React/RCTBridgeModule.h>


@interface ImageProcessor :
NSObject <RCTBridgeModule>
@end


@implementation ImageProcessor


RCT_EXPORT_MODULE();
```

```objc
RCT_EXPORT_METHOD(processImage:(NS
String *)imagePath

callback:(RCTResponseSenderBlock)c
allback)
{
    // Perform image processing
(e.g., resizing, filtering)
    // For simplicity, let's just
return the image path
    callback(@[imagePath]);
}
```

```
@end
```

3. Calling the Native Module in React Native

Once your native module is set up, you can call it from your JavaScript code:

```
javascript
```

```
import { NativeModules } from
'react-native';

const { ImageProcessor } =
NativeModules;

ImageProcessor.processImage('path/
to/image.jpg', (result) => {
    console.log('Processed
Image:', result);
});
```

Using Native Modules for Performance-Heavy Calculations

For tasks like real-time data processing or simulations, using a native module can drastically improve performance, as native code is optimized for these types of operations.

Conclusion

In this chapter, we've explored a variety of performance optimization techniques for React Native apps, including:

- **Profiling your app** using built-in tools like the React Native Performance Monitor and Chrome DevTools.

- **Lazy loading components, optimizing re-renders,** and using tools like React.memo, useCallback, and Suspense to improve app performance.

- **Using native modules** for performance-critical tasks, ensuring that your app can handle complex operations efficiently.

By implementing these techniques, you can significantly enhance the performance of your React Native apps, ensuring they run smoothly even on devices with lower resources.

In the next chapter, we will dive into **Security Best Practices** for React Native, ensuring your app is both secure and reliable. Happy coding, and remember: performance optimization is an ongoing process that pays off by making your app faster and more user-friendly!

Chapter 12: Building for iOS and Android in React Native

Introduction

One of the biggest advantages of React Native is its ability to build cross-platform apps, allowing you to use a single codebase for both iOS and Android. However, while React Native simplifies much of the app-building process, each platform comes with its own set of requirements, tools, and processes. Understanding how to set up and configure the project for each platform is crucial for ensuring that your app runs smoothly across devices.

In this chapter, we will walk through the process of:

- Setting up an iOS project on Xcode.

- Setting up an Android project with Android Studio.

- Running and testing your app on physical devices.

This chapter will provide you with clear, actionable steps and hands-on examples so you can confidently build and deploy your React Native app for both iOS and Android.

---

1. Setting Up an iOS Project on Xcode

Before you can start building your React Native app for iOS, you need to configure the **iOS project** on **Xcode**, which is the integrated development environment (IDE) used for iOS development.

1.1. Prerequisites for iOS Development

Before setting up the project on Xcode, make sure you have the following installed:

- **Xcode**: You need Xcode installed to build iOS apps. You can download it from the Mac App Store.

- **Node.js:** React Native relies on Node.js, which is the runtime for JavaScript. Download it from the official Node.js website.

- **Homebrew**: Homebrew is a package manager for macOS, which can help you install and manage other required dependencies. Install it by running:

bash

```
/bin/bash -c "$(curl -fsSL
https://raw.githubusercontent.com/
Homebrew/install/HEAD/install.sh)"
```

1.2. Installing CocoaPods

CocoaPods is a dependency manager for iOS projects. It's used to install third-party libraries (like React Native dependencies) that are required by your iOS app.

To install CocoaPods, run:

```
bash
```

```
sudo gem install cocoapods
```

1.3. Setting Up Your iOS Project

Once your development environment is set up, the next step is creating your React Native app and setting it up to run on iOS. Follow these steps:

1. **Create a New React Native Project**: Open your terminal and run the following command to create a new React Native project:

```bash
npx react-native init MyProject
```

This will generate the necessary files and directories for your project, including an iOS folder containing the Xcode project.

2. **Navigate to Your Project**: Once the project is created, navigate to the project directory:

```bash
cd MyProject
```

3. **Install iOS Dependencies**: Navigate to the ios directory and install the required dependencies using CocoaPods:

```bash
```

```
cd ios
pod install
cd ..
```

4. **Open the iOS Project in Xcode**: You can open the iOS project by using the following command:

```bash
```

```
open ios/MyProject.xcworkspace
```

This will launch Xcode with the project workspace, where you can configure settings, dependencies, and more.

1.4. Configuring the App for iOS

Before running the app, make sure the following settings are configured in Xcode:

- **App Signing**: Go to the "Signing & Capabilities" tab in Xcode and make sure that your Apple Developer account is selected for signing the app. If you don't have a developer account, you can create one through Xcode or the Apple Developer website.

- **Target Version**: Ensure that the target iOS version is set to an appropriate version that you want your app to support.

1.5. Running the iOS App in Xcode

To run the app on a simulator or a physical device:

1. Choose the target device (e.g., iPhone 12) from the device selection at the top of the Xcode window.

2. Click the **Run** button (a triangle icon) in the top-left corner of Xcode.

3. The app should now launch in the simulator or on the physical device.

2. Setting Up an Android Project with Android Studio

Just as you need Xcode for iOS, you need **Android Studio** for setting up and running Android projects. Android Studio provides the necessary tools to build and test Android apps.

2.1. Prerequisites for Android Development

Before setting up your React Native project for Android, make sure you have the following installed:

- **Android Studio**: Download and install Android Studio from the official website.

- **Java Development Kit (JDK)**: Ensure that JDK 11 or higher is installed. This is required for compiling Android apps.

2.2. Installing Android Studio

1. **Install Android Studio**:

   o Follow the instructions on the Android Studio installation guide to install Android Studio for your operating system.

   o Make sure to install the **Android SDK, Android Virtual Device (AVD)**, and **Android Emulator** during the setup process.

2. **Set Up the Android Emulator**:

o Once Android Studio is installed, open it and go to **Configure > AVD Manager**.

o Create a new Virtual Device by selecting a device (e.g., Pixel 4) and an Android version to install.

o Start the emulator once it's created.

2.3. Configuring Your Android Project

1. **Navigate to Your React Native Project**: If you haven't already, create a new React Native project:

bash

```
npx react-native init MyProject
cd MyProject
```

2. **Install Android Dependencies**: If this is your first time setting up the Android

project, run the following commands to install the necessary dependencies:

```bash
```

```bash
npx react-native run-android
```

3. **Opening the Android Project in Android Studio**: Open the android folder of your React Native project in Android Studio:

```bash
```

```bash
open android
```

This opens the Android project in Android Studio, where you can configure additional settings and dependencies.

2.4. Running the Android App

1. **Running on the Android Emulator:**

   o Make sure your Android Emulator is running.

o In Android Studio, select the device (e.g., Pixel 4) from the device list.

o Click the **Run** button (a green triangle) to launch the app on the emulator.

2. **Running on a Physical Device**: To run the app on a physical device:

o Enable **Developer Options** and **USB Debugging** on your Android device (Settings > About phone > Tap on Build number 7 times).

o Connect the device via USB and make sure it's recognized by Android Studio.

o Run the app as you would on the emulator.

3. Running and Testing on Physical Devices

Testing your app on real devices is crucial, as emulators often don't replicate real-world performance and behavior.

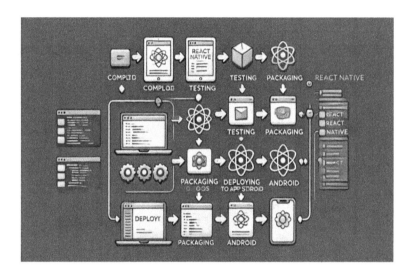

3.1. Running on a Physical iOS Device

1. **Connect Your Device**:

   o Connect your iOS device to your Mac using a USB cable.

- Open Xcode and select your physical device from the device list.

2. **Trust the Developer Profile:**

- If this is your first time running an app on a physical device, you may need to trust your developer profile on the device. Go to **Settings > General > Device Management**, select your developer account, and trust it.

3. **Run the App:**

- Press the **Run** button in Xcode to build and run the app on your physical iOS device.

3.2. Running on a Physical Android Device

1. **Enable Developer Mode and USB Debugging**:

   ○ Go to **Settings > About phone > Tap Build number 7 times** to enable Developer Options.

   ○ Enable **USB Debugging** in **Developer Options**.

2. **Connect Your Device**:

   ○ Connect your Android device to your computer using a USB cable.

3. **Run the App**:

   ○ In Android Studio, select your device from the device list and click **Run** to deploy the app to your physical Android device.

4. Common Issues and Troubleshooting

As you work with React Native and build apps for iOS and Android, you may encounter some common issues. Here are some solutions to frequent problems:

4.1. iOS Build Errors

- **Error: CocoaPods not installed**: If you encounter this error, make sure CocoaPods is installed by running sudo gem install cocoapods and then running pod install inside the ios folder.

- **Xcode version mismatch**: Ensure that your Xcode version is up-to-date with the required version for your React Native project.

4.2. Android Build Errors

- **SDK version mismatch**: If you see errors related to the Android SDK, check your SDK version in **Android Studio** and make sure it matches the version required by React Native.

- **Emulator not launching**: Try restarting the Android Emulator or creating a new virtual device in the **AVD Manager**.

4.3. General Troubleshooting Tips

- **Clear the build cache**: If you encounter strange errors or unexpected behavior, try clearing the build cache:

  - For iOS: cd ios && pod install && cd ..

  - For Android: cd android && ./gradlew clean && cd ..

- **Check device logs**: Use **Xcode logs** for iOS and **Logcat** for Android to get detailed logs of the app's behavior during runtime.

Conclusion

In this chapter, we've covered the entire process of building a React Native app for both iOS and Android. From setting up **iOS projects in Xcode** to configuring **Android projects in Android Studio**, and testing on **physical devices**, you now have the tools and knowledge to build and deploy React Native apps on both platforms.

By following these steps, you can ensure that your app is correctly configured, optimized for performance, and ready to run smoothly on real devices. Understanding how to manage both platforms will give you the flexibility to build high-quality apps for a wide range of users.

In the next chapter, we will dive into **Publishing Your App** to the App Store and Google Play, covering the necessary steps for app submission, optimization, and maintenance. Happy coding!

Chapter 13: Publishing Your App

Introduction

After months of hard work building your React Native app, it's finally time to share it with the world. Publishing your app on the **App Store** for iOS and **Google Play** for Android can be an exciting and rewarding experience. However, the process of preparing your app for release, submitting it to both stores, and managing updates involves a series of steps that need to be carefully followed.

In this chapter, we will walk you through:

- How to prepare for an iOS and Android release.

- Steps for submitting your app to the **App Store** and **Google Play**.

- How to handle app **updates** and **versioning** efficiently.

This chapter will provide a practical, step-by-step approach to get your app ready for the public and ensure it runs smoothly after launch.

---

1. Preparing for an iOS Release

Before you can submit your React Native app to the **App Store**, you need to ensure that it meets all the requirements set by Apple. The preparation process involves configuring your app, creating certificates, and ensuring it's ready for submission.

1.1. Xcode Configuration

To release your app on iOS, you need to configure it properly within **Xcode**, Apple's integrated development environment (IDE).

1. **Set Your App's Version and Build Number:**

   o In Xcode, go to your project settings and select your app target.

   o In the **General** tab, make sure that the **Version** and **Build** numbers are set.

      ▪ **Version:** This is the version number users will see (e.g., 1.0.0).

      ▪ **Build**: This is the internal version number (e.g., 100).

2. **Update the App Icon and Splash Screen:**

- o Ensure that your app's **icon** is correctly set in Xcode. You'll need to provide various sizes for different devices.

- o Set your **launch screen** (splash screen) according to Apple's guidelines.

3. **Code Signing and Certificates:**

- o **Code signing** ensures that your app is trusted by Apple's ecosystem. You'll need to create an **App ID**, **Provisioning Profile**, and **Distribution Certificate** in your **Apple Developer account.**

- o In Xcode, navigate to the **Signing & Capabilities** tab and select your team. Xcode will handle most of the certificate generation automatically.

4. **Enable App Capabilities**: If your app requires specific capabilities (e.g., push notifications, background tasks), ensure that these are enabled in Xcode:

   ○ Go to **Signing & Capabilities** and enable the necessary capabilities (e.g., **Push Notifications** or **In-App Purchases**).

1.2. Test Your App

Testing is crucial before submitting your app to the App Store.

1. **Run on Real Devices**: Test your app on real devices to ensure that it functions as expected on iPhones and iPads.

2. **Use TestFlight**: TestFlight is Apple's beta testing service. It allows you to distribute your app to testers before the official release. Here's how to use it:

- o Upload your app to **App Store Connect.**

- o Add testers (either via email or using public links).

- o Testers can download your app via the TestFlight app on their devices.

1.3. Final Preparations

1. **Create an App Store Connect Account:**

   - o Sign in to **App Store Connect** using your Apple Developer account. This is where you will manage your app's submission.

2. **Prepare Metadata:**

   - o Add your app's name, description, keywords, and other metadata to **App Store Connect.**

- o Upload screenshots of your app for different device sizes (iPhone, iPad, etc.).

3. **App Privacy Policy**:

- o Apple requires you to provide a privacy policy for your app, especially if it collects user data. You can link to your privacy policy hosted online.

---

2. Preparing for an Android Release

Publishing your app to **Google Play** requires similar preparations to iOS, but the process differs in some areas. Let's break down the key steps.

2.1. Setting Up the Android Project

1. **Configure the App's Version:**

   o In your android/app/build.gradle file, set the version code and version name:

```gradle
gradle
```

```gradle
defaultConfig {
    versionCode 1 // Increment
this with each release
    versionName "1.0.0" // Set the
version number
```

```
}
```

2. **Set the App Icon and Splash Screen:**

   o Ensure that your **icon** and **launch screen** are properly set up. You can use a tool like **React Native's react-native-make** to generate the correct icon sizes for Android.

2.2. Create a Keystore for Signing Your App

To sign your Android app, you need a **keystore** file. This is a file that contains your signing keys and ensures your app's integrity.

1. **Generate a Keystore:** Run the following command to generate a new keystore:

```bash
keytool -genkeypair -v -keystore
my-release-key.keystore -keyalg
```

```
RSA -keysize 2048 -validity 10000
-keystore android/app/my-release-
key.keystore
```

Replace my-release-key with your own key name.

2. **Configure the Build Gradle**: Update android/gradle.properties and android/app/build.gradle with your keystore information:

```gradle
gradle
```

```
// android/gradle.properties
MYAPP_RELEASE_STORE_FILE=my-
release-key.keystore
MYAPP_RELEASE_KEY_ALIAS=my-key-
alias
MYAPP_RELEASE_STORE_PASSWORD=*****
MYAPP_RELEASE_KEY_PASSWORD=*****
In android/app/build.gradle:
gradle
```

```
signingConfigs {
    release {
        storeFile
file(MYAPP_RELEASE_STORE_FILE)
        storePassword
MYAPP_RELEASE_STORE_PASSWORD
        keyAlias
MYAPP_RELEASE_KEY_ALIAS
        keyPassword
MYAPP_RELEASE_KEY_PASSWORD
    }
}
```

2.3. Testing Your App on Android

1. **Run on Physical Devices:**

   o Use **USB debugging** to test the app on real Android devices, ensuring it functions correctly across various screen sizes and Android versions.

2. **Android Emulator:**

- o You can also use the **Android Emulator** to test the app on various virtual devices, but real device testing is always recommended for a more accurate representation of performance.

2.4. Google Play Developer Account

Before submitting your app to the **Google Play Store**, you need to create a **Google Play Developer account**. There is a one-time registration fee.

1. **Create an Account:**

   - o Go to Google Play Console and sign up for an account.

2. **Prepare Your App Listing:**

   - o Just like with iOS, provide metadata such as the app name, description, screenshots, and privacy policy.

Make sure you specify the **target audience** and **content rating**.

3. **App Content Policy:**

o Make sure your app complies with Google Play's content policies and guidelines, including ensuring it doesn't violate any right or trademark laws.

---

3. Submitting Your App to the App Store and Google Play

Once you've completed the preparations for both platforms, it's time to submit your app.

3.1. Submitting to the App Store

1. **Upload the App via Xcode:**

- o Open your project in **Xcode** and select **Product > Archive** to create an archive of your app.

- o After the archive is built, Xcode will prompt you to **upload your app** to **App Store Connect.**

2. **App Store Connect:**

- o Once uploaded, go to **App Store Connect** and navigate to the **My Apps** section.

- o Select your app and fill in any missing details, such as metadata, screenshots, and a privacy policy.

- o Submit the app for review by Apple. Apple usually reviews apps within 1-2 days, but it may take longer.

3.2. Submitting to Google Play

1. **Generate a Release APK**:

   o In Android Studio, run the following command to generate a signed **APK**:

```bash
bash
```

```bash
cd android
./gradlew assembleRelease
```

2. **Upload the APK**:

   o Once the **APK** is generated, go to **Google Play Console**, create a new app, and upload your **APK**.

   o Fill out the app's listing, including details, screenshots, and a privacy policy.

3. **Submit for Review**:

   o After filling out the app's details, click **Submit**. Google Play will review the app, which usually takes a few hours, but can take longer.

---

4. Handling App Updates and Versioning

Once your app is live on the App Store and Google Play, it's important to manage app updates and versioning to provide users with bug fixes, improvements, and new features.

4.1. Versioning Your App

Both the App Store and Google Play require proper versioning to handle updates.

- **iOS Versioning:**

  - Update the **version** and **build** numbers in Xcode whenever you make a new release.

  - For a minor update, increment the **build number.**

  - For a major release, increment the **version number.**

- **Android Versioning:**

  - Update the **versionCode** and **versionName** in build.gradle for every release.

```
gradle
```

```
versionCode 2  // Increment this
for each new release
versionName "1.1.0"  // Increment
this for every update
```

4.2. Submitting App Updates

For both iOS and Android:

1. **Prepare the Update**: Make the necessary changes to your app and test thoroughly.

2. **Submit the Update**: Follow the same process as the initial submission for both platforms, but ensure you select the correct version numbers.

3. **Review Process**: Both stores will review your update. Apple generally takes a bit longer than Google Play.

4.3. Managing User Feedback

After releasing an update, monitor user feedback to address issues promptly:

- **iOS**: Use the **App Store Connect** dashboard to view ratings and reviews.

- **Android**: Use **Google Play Console** to monitor feedback.

Respond to user reviews and bugs to improve your app's reputation.

Conclusion

Publishing an app is a significant milestone, but it requires careful preparation and attention to detail. In this chapter, we covered the steps for:

- Preparing your app for release on both **iOS** and **Android**.

- Submitting your app to the **App Store** and **Google Play**.

- Handling updates, versioning, and managing user feedback after launch.

With these steps, you can confidently release your React Native app to the world, ensuring it's both polished and ready for users. In the next chapter, we'll explore **App Marketing and Monetization** to help you grow your user base and generate revenue from your app.

Chapter 14: Real-World Project: To-Do List App

Introduction

Building real-world projects is one of the most effective ways to solidify your understanding of any development framework, and React Native is no exception. In this chapter, we'll guide you through building a **To-Do List app**, a classic beginner project that covers essential concepts such as state management, persistent data storage, and user authentication.

We'll break the project down into clear, digestible steps:

1. **Project Setup**: Setting up the development environment and React Native project.

2. **Coding:** Writing the app code for features like adding, editing, and deleting tasks, as well as handling persistent data storage and user authentication.

3. **Testing:** Writing simple unit tests to ensure the app behaves as expected.

4. **Deployment:** Deploying the app to the **App Store** and **Google Play**, including all the necessary preparation steps.

By the end of this chapter, you will have a fully functional To-Do List app that stores tasks persistently and supports user authentication.

---

1. Project Setup

The first step to building our To-Do List app is setting up the React Native project. We will also need some essential dependencies, including tools for persistent data storage and user authentication.

1.1. Setting Up the React Native Environment

To get started with a new React Native project, we'll need to install some prerequisites, such as **Node.js**, **Watchman**, and the **React Native CLI**. Follow these steps:

1. **Install Node.js**: If you don't already have **Node.js** installed, download and install the

latest version from the official Node.js website.

2. **Install Watchman (macOS only)**: Watchman is a tool developed by Facebook for watching changes in the filesystem. It is necessary for building and running React Native apps.

   o On **macOS**, install Watchman with **Homebrew**:

bash

brew install watchman

3. **Install React Native CLI**: We will use the React Native CLI for project creation:

bash

npm install -g react-native-cli

1.2. Creating the React Native Project

Once the environment is set up, we can create a new React Native project. Run the following command:

```bash
```

```bash
npx react-native init TodoApp
```

This will create a new project folder named **TodoApp** with all the necessary files.

1.3. Installing Dependencies

Next, we'll install some important dependencies to handle data storage and authentication.

1. **AsyncStorage** for persistent data storage (to save the tasks even after the app is closed):

```bash
```

```
npm install @react-native-async-
storage/async-storage
```

2. **Firebase Authentication** for user authentication:

```
bash
```

```
npm install @react-native-
firebase/app @react-native-
firebase/auth
```

3. **React Navigation** for handling app navigation:

```
bash
```

```
npm install @react-
navigation/native @react-
navigation/stack react-native-
screens react-native-safe-area-
context
```

4. **Gesture Handler and Reanimated** (required by React Navigation):

```bash
bash
```

```bash
npm install react-native-gesture-handler react-native-reanimated
```

5. **Link Native Modules**: After installing these libraries, make sure to link the native modules:

```bash
bash
```

```bash
cd ios && pod install && cd ..
```

---

2. Coding the To-Do List App

Now that our environment is set up, we can start coding the features of the To-Do List app. We'll break this down into the following features:

- **Creating and displaying tasks**

- **Persisting tasks with AsyncStorage**

- **Implementing user authentication**

2.1. Setting Up Navigation

We'll use **React Navigation** to manage navigation between the login screen and the main to-do list screen.

1. **Create Navigation Stack**: Inside your App.js, set up the navigation:

```javascript
import React from 'react';
import { NavigationContainer }
from '@react-navigation/native';
import { createStackNavigator }
from '@react-navigation/stack';
import LoginScreen from
'./screens/LoginScreen';
import TodoListScreen from
'./screens/TodoListScreen';

const Stack =
createStackNavigator();
```

```
export default function App() {
    return (
        <NavigationContainer>
            <Stack.Navigator
initialRouteName="Login">
                <Stack.Screen
name="Login"
component={LoginScreen} />
                <Stack.Screen
name="TodoList"
component={TodoListScreen} />
            </Stack.Navigator>
        </NavigationContainer>
    );
}
```

2.2. Building the Login Screen

In this section, we'll create a simple login screen that allows users to sign in or sign up using Firebase Authentication.

1. **Create LoginScreen:** Inside the screens/ folder, create a file LoginScreen.js.

javascript

```javascript
import React, { useState } from
'react';
import { View, TextInput, Button,
Alert, StyleSheet } from 'react-
native';
import auth from '@react-native-
firebase/auth';

export default function
LoginScreen({ navigation }) {
    const [email, setEmail] =
useState('');
    const [password, setPassword]
= useState('');

    const handleLogin = async ()
=> {
```

```
        try {
            await
auth().signInWithEmailAndPassword(
email, password);

navigation.navigate('TodoList');
        } catch (error) {
            Alert.alert('Login
failed', error.message);
        }
    };

    return (
        <View
style={styles.container}>
            <TextInput

style={styles.input}

placeholder="Email"
                value={email}
```

```
onChangeText={setEmail}
          />
             <TextInput

style={styles.input}

placeholder="Password"
                secureTextEntry
                value={password}

onChangeText={setPassword}
          />
             <Button title="Login"
onPress={handleLogin} />
        </View>
      );
}

const styles = StyleSheet.create({
    container: {
```

```
    flex: 1,
    justifyContent: 'center',
    padding: 20,
  },
  input: {
    height: 40,
    borderColor: '#ccc',
    borderWidth: 1,
    marginBottom: 10,
    paddingLeft: 10,
  },
});
```

2.3. Creating the To-Do List Screen

On the **TodoListScreen**, users will be able to add, delete, and view tasks. We will also persist these tasks using **AsyncStorage**.

1. **Create TodoListScreen**: In the screens/ folder, create a file TodoListScreen.js.

javascript

```
import React, { useState,
useEffect } from 'react';
import { View, Text, TextInput,
Button, FlatList,
TouchableOpacity, Alert,
StyleSheet } from 'react-native';
import AsyncStorage from '@react-
native-async-storage/async-
storage';

export default function
TodoListScreen() {
    const [task, setTask] =
useState('');
    const [tasks, setTasks] =
useState([]);

    // Load tasks from
AsyncStorage
    useEffect(() => {
```

```
const loadTasks = async ()
=> {
        const storedTasks =
await
AsyncStorage.getItem('tasks');
        if (storedTasks) {

setTasks(JSON.parse(storedTasks));
        }
    };
    loadTasks();
}, []);

// Save tasks to AsyncStorage
const saveTasks = async
(updatedTasks) => {
        await
AsyncStorage.setItem('tasks',
JSON.stringify(updatedTasks));
        setTasks(updatedTasks);
    };
```

```
// Add a new task
const addTask = () => {
    if (task.trim()) {
        const newTask = { id:
Date.now().toString(), text: task
};
        const updatedTasks =
[...tasks, newTask];

saveTasks(updatedTasks);
        setTask('');
    } else {
        Alert.alert('Please
enter a task.');
    }
};

// Delete a task
const deleteTask = (id) => {
```

```
    const updatedTasks =
tasks.filter((task) => task.id !==
id);
        saveTasks(updatedTasks);
    };


    return (
        <View
style={styles.container}>
            <TextInput

style={styles.input}
                placeholder="Enter
a task"
                value={task}

onChangeText={setTask}
            />
            <Button title="Add
Task" onPress={addTask} />
            <FlatList
```

```
                data={tasks}
                renderItem={({
item }) => (
                    <View
style={styles.task}>

<Text>{item.text}</Text>

<TouchableOpacity onPress={() =>
deleteTask(item.id)}>
                        <Text
style={styles.delete}>Delete</Text
>

</TouchableOpacity>
                    </View>
                )}

keyExtractor={(item) => item.id}
                />
            </View>
```

```
    );
}


const styles = StyleSheet.create({
    container: {
        flex: 1,
        justifyContent: 'center',
        padding: 20,
    },
    input: {
        height: 40,
        borderColor: '#ccc',
        borderWidth: 1,
        marginBottom: 10,
        paddingLeft: 10,
    },
    task: {
        flexDirection: 'row',
        justifyContent: 'space-
between',
        marginBottom: 10,
```

```
    },
    delete: {
        color: 'red',
    },
});
```

Explanation:

- The **TodoListScreen** allows users to add, view, and delete tasks.

- Tasks are stored persistently using **AsyncStorage**, which keeps the tasks even after the app is closed.

- Tasks are displayed using a **FlatList**, which is an efficient way to display a large number of items.

---

3. Testing the App

Now that our app is functional, we'll write some simple tests to ensure it works as expected.

3.1. Writing Unit Tests for Authentication

We can use **Jest** to write unit tests for the login functionality.

1. **Create a test for LoginScreen**: In __tests__/LoginScreen.test.js:

```javascript
import React from 'react';
import { render, fireEvent } from
'@testing-library/react-native';
import LoginScreen from
'../screens/LoginScreen';
import auth from '@react-native-
firebase/auth';

jest.mock('@react-native-
firebase/auth', () => ({
```

```
    signInWithEmailAndPassword:
jest.fn(),
}));


test('LoginScreen allows users to
login', async () => {
    const mockSignIn =
auth().signInWithEmailAndPassword;


mockSignIn.mockResolvedValueOnce({
user: { email: 'test@example.com'
} });


    const { getByText,
getByPlaceholderText } =
render(<LoginScreen />);


fireEvent.changeText(getByPlacehol
derText('Email'),
 'test@example.com');
```

```
fireEvent.changeText(getByPlacehol
derText('Password'),
'password123');


fireEvent.press(getByText('Login')
);



expect(mockSignIn).toHaveBeenCalle
dWith('test@example.com',
'password123');
});
```

3.2. Writing Tests for To-Do List Screen

You can also write tests for the **TodoListScreen** to ensure tasks are added and deleted correctly.

```javascript

import React from 'react';
```

```
import { render, fireEvent } from
'@testing-library/react-native';
import TodoListScreen from
'../screens/TodoListScreen';


test('Adding and deleting tasks',
async () => {
    const { getByPlaceholderText,
getByText, queryByText } =
render(<TodoListScreen />);


    // Adding a task


fireEvent.changeText(getByPlacehol
derText('Enter a task'), 'Buy
groceries');
    fireEvent.press(getByText('Add
Task'));


    // Check if task is added
```

```
expect(getByText('Buy
groceries')).toBeTruthy();

// Deleting a task

fireEvent.press(getByText('Delete'
));

// Check if task is deleted
expect(queryByText('Buy
groceries')).toBeNull();
});
```

4. Deploying the App

Now that the app is functional and tested, it's time to deploy it.

4.1. Deploying to the App Store

1. Create an App Store Connect Account.

2. **Archive the app** in **Xcode** and upload it to **App Store Connect.**

3. **Fill in the app details** (metadata, screenshots, etc.).

4. **Submit the app for review.**

4.2. Deploying to Google Play

1. **Generate a release APK** using Android Studio:

bash

```
cd android
./gradlew assembleRelease
```

2. **Upload the APK** to **Google Play Console.**

3. **Fill in the app details** and **submit** for review.

Conclusion

In this chapter, we built a full-fledged **To-Do List app** that includes authentication, persistent data storage, and the ability to add and delete tasks. We also tested the app and prepared it for deployment on both the **App Store** and **Google Play**.

By working through this project, you've gained practical experience with core React Native concepts, including navigation, authentication, data persistence, and testing. With these skills, you can now build and deploy more complex applications in React Native.

Happy coding, and remember—building real-world projects is the best way to hone your skills!

Chapter 15: Next Steps and Advanced Topics

Introduction

By now, you've become familiar with the fundamentals of React Native, and you may already be building apps that can run on both iOS and Android. However, React Native offers much more to explore as you advance in your development journey. In this chapter, we'll dive into **native modules**, **Expo**, and **TypeScript**, three advanced topics that will help you enhance your app-building skills and make your development process more efficient.

Whether you are a beginner eager to explore more advanced topics, a professional developer looking for better practices, or a hobbyist who wants to deepen your understanding, this chapter will provide you with valuable insights and actionable examples.

By the end of this chapter, you will have a clear understanding of:

- **Native modules**: How to extend React Native with native code and link third-party libraries.

- **Expo**: A toolset for building apps without the hassle of native setup, allowing you to focus more on writing code and less on configuration.

- **TypeScript**: Using TypeScript with React Native to add static typing and improve your app's maintainability and scalability.

Let's get started!

1. Exploring Native Modules and Linking Third-Party Libraries

In React Native, you can create and link **native modules** to access functionality that isn't provided by default in the framework. Native modules are written in platform-specific languages like **Java** (for Android) or **Objective-C/Swift** (for iOS) and allow you to bridge your JavaScript code with the native code of the device.

1.1. What Are Native Modules?

Native modules allow you to write code in the native languages of the mobile operating systems (Android/iOS) and expose that functionality to your React Native JavaScript code. This is useful for accessing platform-specific APIs or functionality that isn't available in React Native out of the box.

For example, if you want to access a device's camera, use native Bluetooth capabilities, or implement complex animations that React Native's JavaScript may not be efficient enough to handle, native modules are a powerful tool.

1.2. Creating a Simple Native Module

Let's create a simple native module that communicates with the device's camera and allows us to capture a photo.

1. **Step 1: Set Up Your React Native Project**

Start by setting up a new React Native project:

bash

npx react-native init NativeModuleExample

cd NativeModuleExample

2. **Step 2: Create the Native Module**

For iOS (Objective-C)

1. In your ios folder, create a new Objective-C file (e.g., CameraModule.m):

```objc
#import <React/RCTBridgeModule.h>

@interface CameraModule : NSObject
<RCTBridgeModule>
@end

@implementation CameraModule

RCT_EXPORT_MODULE();

RCT_EXPORT_METHOD(takePhoto:(RCTResponseSenderBlock)callback)
{
    // Here we would implement
code to interact with the camera
```

```objc
    // For simplicity, just return
a success message
    callback(@[@"Photo taken
successfully"]);
}
```

```
@end
```

2. **Link the Module**: In your AppDelegate.m, add the following import:

`objc`

```objc
#import <React/RCTBridgeModule.h>
```

For Android (Java)

1. In your android/app/src/main/java/com/nativemoduleexample/, create a new Java file (e.g., CameraModule.java):

`java`

```java
package com.nativemoduleexample;

import
com.facebook.react.bridge.ReactApp
licationContext;
import
com.facebook.react.bridge.ReactCon
textBaseJavaModule;
import
com.facebook.react.bridge.ReactMet
hod;
import
com.facebook.react.bridge.Callback
;

public class CameraModule extends
ReactContextBaseJavaModule {

CameraModule(ReactApplicationConte
xt reactContext) {
        super(reactContext);
```

```java
    }

    @Override
    public String getName() {
        return "CameraModule";
    }


    @ReactMethod
    public void takePhoto(Callback
callback) {
        // Here we would interact
with the camera
        // For simplicity, just
return a success message
        callback.invoke("Photo
taken successfully");
    }
}
```

2. **Register the Module:** In MainApplication.java, register the module:

```java
java
```

```
import
com.nativemoduleexample.CameraModu
le;

@Override
protected List<ReactPackage>
getPackages() {
    return
Arrays.<ReactPackage>asList(
        new MainReactPackage(),
        new CameraModule() // Add
this line
    );
}
```

1.3. Calling the Native Module from JavaScript

Now that the native module is created, you can call it from your JavaScript code in **React Native**.

1. **Access the Native Module in JavaScript**: In your App.js:

```javascript
import React from 'react';
import { Button, Alert } from
'react-native';
import { NativeModules } from
'react-native';

const { CameraModule } =
NativeModules;

const App = () => {
    const takePhoto = () => {

CameraModule.takePhoto((message)
=> {
            Alert.alert(message);
        });
    };
```

```
return (
    <Button title="Take Photo"
onPress={takePhoto} />
    );
};
```

```
export default App;
```

This code allows you to call the takePhoto method from your native module, triggering the device's camera functionality (which would be implemented in the native code).

1.4. Using Third-Party Libraries

You may need to use third-party libraries that provide native code to extend React Native's capabilities. To link such libraries, you can follow these steps:

1. **Install the Library**:

```bash
bash
```

```
npm install <library-name>
```

2. **Link the Library**: React Native generally links libraries automatically (especially in recent versions). If it doesn't, use:

```bash
```

```
npx react-native link <library-
name>
```

3. **Configure Native Code**: Sometimes, third-party libraries require additional setup in native code (e.g., modifying MainApplication.java for Android or AppDelegate.m for iOS).

2. Overview of Expo for Building Apps Without Native Setup

Expo is a framework and platform for universal React applications that can help you build apps without needing to worry about native setup. It provides a managed environment where you don't need to deal with configuring iOS or Android projects manually.

2.1. What is Expo?

Expo simplifies the React Native development experience by providing tools that manage complex native code configurations for you. With Expo, you don't need to worry about setting up Xcode, Android Studio, or dealing with the complexities of native modules.

2.2. Creating a New Expo Project

Creating a new Expo project is simple and quick. To get started:

1. **Install Expo CLI**: If you haven't already, install **Expo CLI** globally:

bash

```
npm install -g expo-cli
```

2. **Create a New Expo Project**: To create a new Expo project, run:

bash

```
expo init MyNewApp
cd MyNewApp
```

3. **Start the Project**: Run the app in your browser or on a physical device:

bash

```
expo start
```

2.3. Benefits of Using Expo

- **No Need for Native Code Setup**: Expo handles all the complexities of native setup for you, meaning you don't need to use Android Studio or Xcode.

- **Fast Development**: Expo offers features like **hot reloading** and **live preview**, making it easier to build and test your app.

- **Pre-Built Components**: Expo includes a set of pre-built UI components, APIs, and tools that can speed up your development process, such as **push notifications**, **camera**, and **location services**.

- **Easy Deployment**: Expo makes it easier to deploy your app without needing to deal with certificates, provisioning profiles, or configuring app stores.

2.4. Limitations of Expo

While Expo is great for many use cases, it does have limitations:

- **Custom Native Modules**: Expo doesn't support all native modules, so if you need to use a specific native feature that Expo doesn't support, you may need to eject from Expo.

- **App Size**: Because Expo includes many features by default, your app may become larger than a custom React Native app.

2.5. Ejecting from Expo

If you need full control over your project or need to use a native module that Expo doesn't support, you can **eject** your app from Expo. To eject, run:

```bash
```

```
expo eject
```

This will generate native iOS and Android projects, and you'll have full control over the project setup.

---

3. Introduction to Using React Native with TypeScript

TypeScript is a statically typed superset of JavaScript that adds type safety to your code. Using TypeScript with React Native can help you catch errors early in development, improve code maintainability, and make your app more scalable.

3.1. Setting Up TypeScript in a React Native Project

1. **Create a New React Native Project:** Start by creating a new React Native project as usual:

```bash
bash
```

```bash
npx react-native init MyTSApp
```

2. **Install TypeScript**: Install TypeScript and the necessary type definitions:

```bash
bash
```

```bash
npm install --save-dev typescript
@types/react @types/react-native
```

3. **Configure TypeScript**: Create a tsconfig.json file in the root of your project:

```json
json
```

```json
{
  "compilerOptions": {
    "target": "es5",
    "lib": ["es6", "dom"],
    "allowJs": true,
    "skipLibCheck": true,
    "esModuleInterop": true,
```

```
  "strict": true,
  "jsx": "react-native"
},
"exclude": ["node_modules"]
}
```

4. **Rename Files to .ts and .tsx**: Rename your JavaScript files (.js) to TypeScript files (.ts or .tsx for React components).

3.2. Benefits of Using TypeScript with React Native

- **Type Safety**: TypeScript helps prevent common bugs by checking types and providing clear error messages during development.

- **IntelliSense**: Most modern code editors, such as **VS Code**, provide **IntelliSense** for TypeScript, making it easier to work with APIs and third-party libraries.

- **Improved Refactoring**: With type safety in place, refactoring becomes easier and less error-prone.

3.3. Example of TypeScript in React Native

Here's an example of a simple React Native component written in TypeScript:

```tsx
import React, { useState } from
'react';
import { View, Text, Button,
StyleSheet } from 'react-native';

interface CounterProps {
  initialCount?: number;
}
```

```
const Counter:
React.FC<CounterProps> = ({
initialCount = 0 }) => {
  const [count, setCount] =
useState<number>(initialCount);

  const increment = () =>
setCount(count + 1);
  const decrement = () =>
setCount(count - 1);

  return (
    <View
style={styles.container}>
      <Text>{count}</Text>
      <Button title="Increment"
onPress={increment} />
      <Button title="Decrement"
onPress={decrement} />
    </View>
  );
```

```
};


const styles = StyleSheet.create({
  container: {
    flex: 1,
    justifyContent: 'center',
    alignItems: 'center',
  },
});


export default Counter;
```

3.4. Debugging TypeScript in React Native

When working with TypeScript, debugging can be easier because the compiler checks for errors before the code even runs. If you encounter an error, TypeScript will often provide a helpful message about what went wrong, making it easier to fix the issue quickly.

Conclusion

In this chapter, we've explored several advanced topics that will take your React Native development skills to the next level:

- **Native Modules**: How to extend React Native with native code and link third-party libraries.

- **Expo**: A platform that simplifies app development by handling much of the native setup for you.

- **TypeScript**: Using TypeScript to improve your app's maintainability, scalability, and code quality.

These topics open up new possibilities for building powerful and efficient apps with React Native. By incorporating these tools and techniques, you can take on more complex projects and become a more versatile React Native developer.

In the next chapter, we will dive into **Advanced Performance Optimization**, focusing on techniques for making your React Native apps faster and more efficient.

Happy coding!